Dream Me Home Safely

Dream Me Home Safely

Edited by
SUSAN RICHARDS SHREVE

Foreword by
MARIAN WRIGHT EDELMAN

A MARINER ORIGINAL

Houghton Mifflin Company

BOSTON   NEW YORK   2003

For information about permission to reproduce selections from
this book, write to Permissions, Houghton Mifflin Company,
215 Park Avenue South, New York, New York 10003.

Visit our Web site: www.houghtonmifflinbooks.com.

Library of Congress Cataloging-in-Publication Data is available.
ISBN 0-618-37902-9

Book design by Anne Chalmers
Typefaces: Janson Text, Humanist, and Type Embellishments

PRINTED IN THE UNITED STATES OF AMERICA
QUM 10 9 8 7 6 5 4 3 2 1

"Ars Politica" by Julia Alvarez. Copyright © 2003 by Julia Alvarez. Reprinted by permission of Susan Bergholz Literary Services, New York.

"The Center of the Universe" by Tina McElroy Ansa. Copyright © 2003 by Tina McElroy Ansa. Reprinted by permission of the author.

"My Father's Dance" by Robert Bausch. Copyright © 2003 by Robert Bausch. Reprinted by permission of the author.

"from *Sweet Summer*" by Bebe Moore Campbell. Copyright © 1989 by Bebe Moore Campbell. First published in *Sweet Summer: Growing Up With and Without My Dad* (Putnam). Reprinted by permission of the author.

"Rowing in Amboy" by Alan Cheuse. Copyright © 2003 by Alan Cheuse. Reprinted by permission of the author.

"Thread" by Stuart Dybek. Copyright © 2003 by Stuart Dybek. Reprinted by permission of the author.

"Parenthood: A Life Sentence" by Patricia Elam. Copyright © 2003 by Patricia Elam. Reprinted by permission of the author.

"A Child's Garden of Verse" by Carolyn Ferrell. Copyright © 2003 by Carolyn Ferrell. Reprinted by permission of the author.

"from *The Kingdom of Brooklyn*" by Merrill Joan Gerber. Copyright © Merrill Joan Gerber. First published in *The Kingdom of Brooklyn* (Longstreet Press). Reprinted by permission of the author.

CONTENTS

FOREWORD

I am so grateful for this book celebrating the Children's Defense Fund's thirtieth anniversary. This gift of thirty-four extraordinary American writers sharing their stories of growing up in America paints a complex, richly detailed, and achingly real portrait of American childhood. Every reader will catch glimpses of his or her own childhood and see the childhoods of others with new eyes.

Tina McElroy Ansa remembers her nurturing black Georgia family and community as a world "made up of stories," and listening at her mother's side "as she whipped up batter for one of her light-as-air, sweet-as-mother's-love desserts." In a town on Chicago's North Shore, Mary Morris learns early on how girls and women can get into "trouble," while boys and men escape blame — and, since she is a girl, she makes an exit plan, just in case. Michael Patrick MacDonald sees his father's face for the first time at his funeral and leaves the service with a renewed appreciation for the family he does have and the unspoken community of love and loyalty that surrounds him in his poor and desperate "white trash" South Boston neighborhood: "For once in my life I felt I should be proud of where I came from, who I was, and who I might become, and for a moment was ashamed for having ever felt otherwise." Lois-Ann Yamanaka writes about trying not to panic when the autistic son she loves so fiercely sees balloons in the supermarket checkout line, knowing the moment is about to escalate into a fit of frustrated screaming and thrashing that will force her to drag him from the store while other customers stare in disgust: "In JohnJohn's world, I can afford to buy him every balloon on every trip to the market. In JohnJohn's world, he takes all of the shiny balloons home to our yard full of white ginger blossoms and lets all of them go . . . [a] moment of beauty, his silent freedom."

Anna Quindlen looks at the overscheduled lives of today's children and mourns what's been lost: "Pickup games. Hanging out. How boring it was. Of course, it was the making of me, as a human being and a writer. Downtime is where we become ourselves, looking into the middle distance, kicking at the curb, lying on the grass or sitting on the stoop and staring at the tedious blue of the summer sky. I don't believe you can write poetry or compose music or become an actor without downtime, and plenty of it, a hiatus that passes for boredom but is really the quiet moving of the wheels inside that fuel creativity." Alan Cheuse writes about his especially fortunate circumstances growing up on the water: "I don't know how it would have been, born into a town without a coastline . . . The ebb and flow of waters, the detritus, flotsam, treasures left behind on the sand, the marine life, fresh water and salt mingling in the tides, the sound of buoys on summer nights, bells, horns, the ships anchored within sight of our playlands: the hope this gives you as a child, there is almost no explaining." And in another world, Julia Alvarez dreams of someday being able to turn her life story into a book another little girl might want to read — "a girl like me, no longer frightened by / the whisperings of terrified adults, / the cries of uncles being rounded up, / the sirens of the death squads racing by."

As singular as every one of these stories of childhood is, common threads run through them, linking experiences across race, class, and geography. The role of many memorable adults who stand up for children is striking. I hope readers will recognize people like them in their own lives: Alexs Pate's mother, determined that her son will not be mistreated by teachers or led to believe he is destined to be a "negative statistic," on yet another determined march to the principal's office in his defense; Anthony Grooms's mother putting him and his sister to bed at Christmas to the sounds of Burl Ives and Nat King Cole; Robert Bausch's father pretending to wake his six children up on Christmas morning by blaring Benny Goodman or Glenn Miller on the hi-fi; Jeanne Wakatsuki Houston's and Bich Minh Nguyen's grandmothers, suspicious of the neighbors, the children's friends, the toadstools in the front yard — any of the pieces of the outside world that might somehow bring their family harm. And John Edgar Wideman's mother, sitting at her apartment window watching for the child out way too late, prepared to wait up as long as it takes to dream him home safely.

Reading these stories, we may wonder what our children will remember about us. Will we be remembered for doing everything we could to dream them home safely? Even ideal childhoods are marked with some degree of fear and uncertainty. Scary movies, bullies, illness, and death are timeless. But while generations throughout history have often looked back to the times before them as simpler and more innocent, in many ways childhood today may be more dangerous than ever. Pervasive cultural, domestic, and community violence, child abuse and neglect, drugs, high rates of hunger and homelessness, and tenuous family and community supports ravage the lives and dreams of countless young people. Community breakdown has coincided with a culture saturated with violence- and sex-filled images, and too many parents seek to meet children's needs with things rather than time. Too many children are left alone to sort out the values promoted relentlessly by television, movies, and video games. Safety nets for children and families are being eroded as politicians place millionaires' desires before children's needs. And year by year it seems as if adults' hold on our children's hands and values is becoming looser and looser, so that too many children sink in the quicksand of materialism and spiritual poverty.

There are sad stories and painful memories in this collection, but also a great deal of hope, as seen in children's resilience, their small kindnesses to other children, the writers' ability to look back through the lens of time at the parents and siblings and houses and neighborhoods they were given and understand what true gifts these things were. And with all their accumulated flaws, the adults in these essays sometimes appear at their best, too, in stories of parents who hold on to their children through minor crises and major catastrophes, refusing to let go. May each reader learn to do the same for every one of our children, until collectively and individually we are able to dream them *all* home safely.

I am so grateful to the wonderful writers who have generously shared their talents and childhood experiences here. Profound thanks are due to Tim Seldes; to Susan Shreve, who made this book happen; to Susan Watts, who coordinated this effort; to Deanne Urmy, our very able editor; and, as always, to Martha Espinosa and Lisa Clayton Robinson, who provided me with invaluable assistance.

MARIAN WRIGHT EDELMAN

Dream Me
Home Safely

JULIA ALVAREZ

 Ars Politica

I was the daughter who changed overnight
from clingy, thumb in her mouth, a problem child,
always afraid and needing to be soothed
to feisty, elbows-out, watch-out-for-her!
What happened — so the family story tells —
was that I picked up reading and began
to make things up, to take the hurricane
out of the wind, bring back the disappeared,
replace the shanty shacks with palaces,
and turn the beggars loose on my vegetables.

I yearned to write the story of my life
into a book a girl might want to read,
a girl like me, no longer frightened by
the whisperings of terrified adults,
the cries of uncles being rounded up,
the sirens of the death squads racing by
towards a destination I could change
with an eraser or a trick ending.
There had to be a way to make the world
safer . . . so we could bear to live in it!

This might not be the destiny of art,
to save the uncles, free the prisoners
in a storybook, but it's a start —

my start, *our* start, if Wordsworth had it right,
and the child is the father of the man.
The inhumanity of our humanity
will not be fixed by metaphor alone.
The plot will fail, the tortured will divulge
our names, our human story end, unless
our art can right what happens in the world.

TINA McELROY ANSA

The Center of the Universe

On the way home from school one day when I was seven or eight years old — a black child growing up in Macon, Georgia, in the 1950s — my father, Walter McElroy, took me to a huge fountain in a city park. At the edge of the fountain, he pointed to the water and said very seriously, "That is the exact center of Georgia."

It was a momentous revelation for me. Since that instant, I have always thought of myself being at the center of my universe, enveloped in the world around me. From that day, I have imagined myself standing at that fountain surrounded by my African American community of Pleasant Hill, in my hometown of Macon, in middle Georgia, with the muddy Ocmulgee River running nearby, with the entire state of Georgia around me, then all of the southeastern section of the continental United States, then the country, the Western Hemisphere, then the world.

The image has always made me feel safe. Sheltered by my surroundings, enveloped in the arms of "family" of one kind or another, mostly southern family. That is how I see myself, a southerner.

For some folks, my discussing my southernness makes them downright uncomfortable. I mean really, the very idea, a black person, an African American over the age of thirty-five, going on and on about the South and her place in it as if she weren't aware of the region, its past, and all it stands for.

Doesn't she know history? she seems to think. And she's a writer, too. It's almost embarrassing.

As if a black person does not belong in the South, to the South. In a couple of decades of moving up and down the United States' eastern seaboard, I found there was no place else I *did belong*.

Of course I know the region's history, I want to tell folks looking askance at me. I know it because I am a part of the history. My parents were part of that history. And their parents were part of it.

My father's people came from Wrightsville, in the south-central part of the state. They were farming people, like most black people at the turn of the twentieth century. At that time, black folks owned nearly twenty million acres of farmland in the United States. When my father's father, Frank, left the farm nearly one hundred years ago for the city of Macon and work on the M-D-S — the Macon-Dublin-Savannah train line, which connected those three Georgia cities — his brother Isadore (whom we called "Uncle Sunshine") and his family remained there on the farm. As a child, when my parents, two older brothers and two older sisters, and I piled into our green woodie station wagon and left the "city" for a few days in summer to visit the "country," it was to Uncle Sunshine's farm we went.

My mother's people — the Lees — were also from middle Georgia. But they were "city people," they were not farmers. They were schoolteachers and tradespeople and semiprofessionals. Everyone in town knew my great-grandfather as "Pat, the barber." All I have to do now is say that name to make my mother smile with nostalgia and begin telling me stories surrounding the antique red leather barbershop chair that sat on my great-aunt's back porch for decades. Patrick Lee's maiden daughter, Elizabeth, not only took over her father's barbershop when he died in the 1930s. She also taught folks in middle Georgia from the cradle to the grave. During the day, she led her own private kindergarten class. During the evenings, she taught illiterate adults to read. "All I want to do is learn to read the Bible," they would tell her. She always chuckled: "Lord, some of the most difficult words and concepts in the world are in the Bible."

In childhood, I always thought of her as just a stern religious old maid who didn't even drink Coca-Colas or take aspirin because they were "dope" or let you sleep in any bed in her house past sunup lest you get "the big head." I thank the Holy Spirit that she and I both lived long enough for me to see her for the extraordinary African American woman that she was. She was one of the reasons my mother loved reading and passed that love on to her children.

Today, every word I write, I write on a computer atop the old pedal-motored Singer sewing machine console that once sat in Auntie's bedroom.

It is no wonder that in my childhood family house — a big old brick two-story house with an attic and basement — there were books everywhere: in the bedrooms, the bathroom, the living room, and the kitchen. When I was a child, the joke in our family was to shove a copy of the tiny Macon telephone book under the door of the bathroom when someone hollered out for some new reading material. Whenever that happened to me, I happily sat there with my legs dangling off the toilet and amused myself by reading that phone book, looking up my friends' numbers and addresses, coming upon interesting names, making up stories about the people and streets I encountered there.

When I was growing up, I thought the entire world was made up of stories. My mother gossiping on the phone was to my ear my mother weaving stories. The tales of love and woe that I overheard from the customers at my father's juke joints and liquor store down on Broadway and Mulberry Street, as I sat at the end of the bar in my Catholic school uniform doing my homework, were to me stories. My grandfather Walter McElroy's ghost stories of cats wearing diamond rings sticking their hands into blazing campfires. My Baptist great-auntie Elizabeth Lee relating how she always wanted to go to the Holy Land but had no intention of crossing any water to get there. My mother telling me over and over as she whipped up batter for one of her light-as-air, sweet-as-mother's-love desserts how she made her first cake when she was only seven.

I draw sustenance from these stories, in the same way I draw nourishment from knowing that my father's people farmed land right up the road in Wrightsville, Georgia. In my southern mind, I can see Uncle Sunshine drawing his bony mule under the hot shade of a tall Georgia pine and wiping his brow when I gaze at the pine trees around my house. I never cross a railroad track without recalling my grandfather's years with the M-D-S line and the first time my father put me on the famed "Nancy Hanks" train for a trip to Savannah by myself. After my father handed me over to the care of the train's porters, they asked, pointing to my father's retreating back, "Who was that boy?" I replied indignantly, "That's no boy! That's my daddy!" The black men looked at each other and just beamed. Then proceeded to getting me cold Coca-Colas and sneaking me sandwiches from the whites-only dining car. For the rest of the four-hour trip, they treated me like a princess, heaping on me the loving attention usually thought of as the preserve of little white girls traveling on the southern train system. In fact, they treated me better. They treated me like family.

Family. As a writer, a novelist, it is all that I write about. My first novel, *Baby of the Family*, is not just about my retaining that special place of the last born in my household. It is also about the ties, the connections, the stories, the food, the rituals, the seasons, the minutiae that go into forming the family unit.

Like all of us, I carry my childhood with me.

No matter where I go or in what time zone I find myself, at eleven o'clock Eastern Standard Time Sunday mornings, I think of St. Peter Claver Church sitting at the top of Pleasant Hill and the sacrament of the Eucharist being celebrated there. Sunday morning mass in my childhood parish is still the quintessential Sunday morning to me. Just as that fountain in the middle of Tatnall Square Park is the primary bellwether for my place in the universe.

When I write, I still envision myself standing at that fountain surrounded by my family, my community, my hometown, my state, my country, and the world.

From time to time, my mother will wistfully remind some old friend of hers who asks about me, "Tina doesn't live in Macon anymore."

My Mama is right. I *don't* live in Macon anymore.

Macon lives in me.

ROBERT BAUSCH

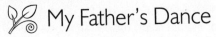 My Father's Dance

On my desk is a picture of my father, age seventy-two or so, in his pale blue pajamas, wearing a round-topped, one-inch-brimmed white hat and dancing with his great-grandson, Brandon. My father is really dancing, a wide grin on his face, his hand outstretched, holding on to the little boy's hand. Brandon is my niece's son, probably six or seven years old when this picture was taken. He's doing the best he can for a little guy, but mostly he's just standing there, watching my father. At least it doesn't appear that the boy is dancing. My father is in bare feet, one foot high in the air, as he kicks to the music. I know, without having been there, what song he is dancing to. It is "One O'Clock Jump," by Benny Goodman. The fact that I know that, that I can look at the picture and hear the music, and that everyone in the picture is smiling or laughing, is a measure of what I remember from my childhood.

The only thing missing from the picture is my mother. She has been dead for at least five years when this picture is taken, and my father is still, as we came to see later, grieving her loss. Now he is dead too. He's been gone for almost a decade himself. They were best friends and lovers for fifty-five years. They raised six of us — four boys and two girls. We were all grown and gone when, in 1974, my sister Barbara — their oldest daughter — was killed with her husband in an automobile accident. My mother and father raised their four children. Later, when Barbara's daughter Laura decided to end an unhappy marriage, she and her son,

Brandon, moved back home with my father. In the picture on my desk, Brandon is dancing with his "Daddy." That's what he always called my father. Three generations of children in my family have called him that. Two generations called my mother "Mommy."

I grew up in a terrific, big, loud, happy family. We fought, bickered, laughed, teased, betrayed, cried, and screamed at each other; we also begged forgiveness and hugged each other, for all the days of my childhood. I lived in that family, then watched as my sister's four children, after her death, became a part of a new family with my mother and father — a different family. They, too, had their traditions, their joys and woes, wild crazy fun, and loud, furious fights. They, too, loved each other and still get together as much as they can as grownups. I was their uncle in the beginning, but now feel more like an older brother; one who left home too soon, and missed out on their formidable years. I watched Laura and Brandon become yet a third family with its own traditions and remembered stories of tension and stress, laughter and joy.

But I know what it was mostly like.

I know because our family always had traditions, immutable laws of behavior based on one basic and unalterable truth: family came first. Always. It was simply your duty to honor the people you were supposed to love.

The process of learning that was sometimes painful. My mother would say no when I wanted to go with my friends to a movie, or over to play pool at the local pool hall, or just to stay home and be by myself for a while, to read books and pretend I had no siblings in whose needs I had to take an interest. It all seemed so completely unfair to me. I never wanted to spend a whole day at home, squirming with my brothers and sisters because my Aunt Florence was coming over, or because it was Barbara's birthday. Or just because "your father wants you here. He never sees you anymore."

Once, I was in my room, reading a book, and my father opened the door and said, "Hey, you want to go shoot some baskets?"

I was shocked that he asked me. He worked so hard, he hardly had time for things like that. And I had been running with my friends mostly. I never had time for him and, more important, never wanted time with him. I said, "No, I really don't." It was late fall, and chilly outside. I didn't want to be out in that air. I didn't want to be around anyone who had such authority over me as my father had. Mostly I tried to avoid him. That day, all I wanted was to stay home and read.

He seemed disappointed. He closed the door and went away, and I felt a pang of regret for having rejected him, but it wasn't enough to get me out of that bed. My mother did that. When my father was outside, by himself, shooting hoops, she came in and scolded me. "What are you thinking of?" she said. "Get out there and play ball with your dad." It turned out to be one of the best times with him — one of those times you remember for the sheer fun of it, not for what it meant to you. We just had fun together. My brother Dick joined us and we played a whole afternoon under a gray sky. I never felt cold, although I remember I could see my breath.

Still, I fought with my mother at every turn whenever she said, "It's your family. What's more important?" I harbored secret enmity in my heart for my father whenever he said, "She's your mother. Honor her. Get in there and help with the dishes."

It was so unfair to me. I'd have to clean up a huge mess I didn't even make. Or I'd get thrown in with somebody who was doing that. With six of us, my mother always had plenty of help with the dishes. There was just too much noise in that small house for me. Too many people to take into account. I wanted to be out of there, running with my friends, doing things I wanted to do, without consideration of anyone else. Or that's what I believed. Mostly, I now see, I wanted to please my friends, but I would have denied it vehemently at the time. I didn't think I wanted to see to the needs of anyone but myself.

"Your sister has the flu," my mother would say. "You're going to have to help take care of her."

"I am?"

"She's very sick."

I felt nothing. I knew I didn't have it. I'd never had it. Our doctor said, "Some folks are immune, I guess." As long as I couldn't get the flu, I was happy. My mother got it all the time. If one of the children came down with it, she was almost guaranteed to be bedridden for several days if she got anywhere near the stricken party. So she decided the one who didn't get it would take care of the ones who did. (I was in my thirties the first time I knew what it felt like to get the flu. And once I knew, I understood completely why my mother wanted to avoid getting it.)

"Take your sister some soup," my mother would say, and she'd hand me a bowl of steaming chicken noodle soup. Like the soup, the noodles were homemade. She'd spend a whole morning flattening a flour, egg, and water mixture, rolling it up and very carefully cutting it into thin slices, then unrolling each one until she had these wonderful egg noodles with creases in them where they had been folded. She'd put them in the soup at the last minute, stir it until the noodles were just cooked, then she'd pour the whole thing over a pile of mashed potatoes. She called it Chicken Mash. "This will make your sister feel better." When I tell people this story, they picture an old woman leaning over a stove. But she was young then. Young and beautiful. People used to say she was a dead ringer for Maureen O'Hara.

I was always nominated to feed the sick, because as I said, I never knew what the flu felt like until I was full-grown. But I hated that house when everyone had the flu. I had to stay home, watch the suffering through what seemed like a gray wall of air; I'd carry food to the stricken, add water to the cool mist humidifiers, and put cool towels on hot foreheads. This was not trauma, but it felt like it because I had such a powerful longing to escape.

The thing I remember most about my family, though — and perhaps this is because as I write this, another Christmas approaches — is what it was like on Christmas mornings. I think the picture of my father dancing was taken around Christmas. I'd be willing to bet on it, although I know it's possible it was in the dead of summer. He danced with Brandon a lot over the years.

What I remember about Christmas mornings is a small square of space most people would call a hallway that opened into our dining room. It was right outside the bedroom doors in that small house on Valleywood Drive in Wheaton, Maryland. My two sisters, Barbara and Betty, stayed in the first room on the right as you entered the hall from the dining room. Right next to their room, on the same wall, was our room. The boys. Tim, Steve, Richard, and me. We had bunk beds. Richard and I slept on the top bunks, Steve and Tim on the bottom. Directly next to our room, the wall turned, facing the dining room entrance and forming the third side of the square. On that wall was a small linen closet, then the entrance to my parents' bedroom. On the fourth side of the square was the bathroom door, and then another long space of wall before it ended at the dining room entrance. My father would get out of bed early, walk unsteadily to that small, square space, and listen for the measured breathing of his children. I know this because I was never asleep. I don't believe any of us were. When he was sure we couldn't hear him, he would sneak into the living room, lift the lid on top of the hi-fi set, and turn it on. He would have already placed a record on the turntable of Benny Goodman's "One O'Clock Jump." Or sometimes he'd play Glenn Miller's "Pennsylvania 6-5000" or "In the Mood." Whatever the selection, he would have already had it set to the highest volume. The blast of music would be intended to wake all of us up. He'd come back to the little square in front of our bedroom doors and wait for us. My mother would get out of bed and put on her robe and be standing there too, her arms folded in front of her as if to hold her robe closed, her red hair flowing down her back, her bright green eyes smiling. We all had to stay away from the dining room entrance when we came out. We could not look through into the living room yet. Dad would make us line up against the wall in front of Barbara and Betty's room. Steve and Tim would be so excited, whispering was impossible, but we all tried. As though we didn't want to wake up the rest of the world. It was impossible for those two boys to stand still, but we all had to line up against the wall in front of Barbara and Betty's room. From the smallest to the tallest. I was always in back with my brother Richard. Then Barbara was in front of us, Betty in front of her, Steve in front of Betty, and little Timmy first in line. We ranged in height from a little over two feet (Timmy, for a while there; he is now the tallest member of our family, at six feet two) right up to five feet eleven inches.

For a few years, in the beginning, Barbara was the last in line, but Dick and I eventually outgrew her. What I remember, more than the order, was the ritual. We all had to line up first, while the music played. Then my mother and father would put their arms around each other and follow us as we walked slowly into the living room.

I have pictures too, I'm sure, of the chaos and mess we made those mornings. The piles of wrapping paper and boxes and plastic bubble wrap. I remember those days, those Christmas days, now with so much joy and with the ache of remembered love. I don't recall a thing I got on any of those Christmases. Some years were leaner than others. It's possible that on some holiday mornings I didn't manage to get a thing I had wished for. I really don't remember. Because every one of those mornings, and all the other days and hours growing up in that family, I was given the greatest gift of all: the one that destroys meanness in you; the one that provides a sense of the beauty in people and the essence of loving and caring for others; the one that makes you aware of loveliness and the ephemeral, yet lasting nature of joy; the one you take for granted all through the many years of being too busy to say what it meant to you. Only now — now when it's too late — I wish I could say to my mother and father how much I appreciate them and how fortunate I am because I was lucky enough to be in that family.

I have a family of my own now. And they're mostly grown. I'm hoping for a grandchild soon. I've tried to teach what I learned all those years in my mother and father's house, all those things I didn't realize I was learning and that I never knew I'd be so grateful for. When you have love and it's proffered every day in a kind of tender, yet stern insistence and even reckless laughter, when it is given to you and you accept it in life as a thing as natural as rain or snow, or the litter of leaves in fall, you can't help but take it for granted. For a bewildered while you incorrectly understand that the world has given you this because it's there in equal measure, everywhere. You never know, until it's too late to do anything about it, how sweet the effort is: how lasting the human will to love can be in the breast of people who want to make it for *you*, who want to give it to *you*, without calculating what's in it for them, without thinking at all of what it will mean when you grow to full adulthood, see the world as it is, and forget to mention what you have been given.

Every day of my grown-up life, I have wanted to do what my parents did. I have wanted to widen the province of love and weaken hate and bitterness in the hearts of my children. And I've done these things because of what I got from my family, all those lovely years when I was growing up, being loved and cherished and, unbeknown to me, and in the best way, honored, for myself.

What greater gift is there?

So now, whenever I look at this picture on my desk I remember all those years I was my father's son; I remember my mother's laugh, and the way she made me think of somebody other than myself; I think of my brothers and sisters, nieces and nephews, and all of their children; I remember my own children and all the years of loving and cherishing them, and I realize that in spite of change and sadness and loss, in spite of the withering passage of time, my father is still dancing.

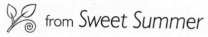 from *Sweet Summer*

Feathers flying, wings beating hard, squawking like a wild banshee, the chicken streaked past Grandma's outstretched hands, away from the back porch and across the barnyard. *Whooosh!* Grandma slammed the door real fast, trapping the remaining two birds inside the rickety coop. Slowly she stood up. She let her arms hang loose next to her body for a moment and made a faint, wordless sound, not even a sigh. A summoning. Then she slowly lumbered past the pump, into the small wooden shed that served as the smokehouse, picked up a large ax hanging on the wall, and plodded after the feathered escapee. I trailed right behind her.

Grandma had been fattening the three hens for several weeks, isolating them from the other chickens, who had the run of the henhouse and the yard. She fed the birds nothing but corn kernels and water. "You gotsta clean out chickens, 'cause no tellin' what all nasty stuff they be eatin'" is what Grandma told me the day she snatched the three unsuspecting chickens — bip, bam, bip — lightning fast; before they could even squawk they were in the cage. Now the three birds were plump and ready for the frying pan. But first Grandma would have to catch them.

Her large, bare feet dragged through the dirt as she tracked the chicken across the yard. Grandma never wore shoes unless she was going out of the lane, which most weeks meant only Sundays. The soles of her feet were as tough and hard as leather. She was a big woman, very wide and sturdy. She reached in one of the pockets of her dress, pulled out a handkerchief, wiped at her nose, then put the handkerchief away. Thin lines crisscrossed her high cheekbones, her forehead, and under her eyes, reflecting her almost seventy years. As she walked her long, silky braid dangled down her back.

"You gonna get 'em, Grandma?" I asked, excitedly watching the frantic chicken race across the yard in the direction of Grandma's vegetable garden.

"You sure you wanna see this, Bebe? Gone be bloody and I don't want you gettin' scared and hoppin' and hollerin' and havin' nightmares and all."

"I'm not gonna be scared, Grandma. It's gonna be fun."

"That's what you call it, huh?"

Sure it was fun! The only chickens I saw in Philly were the frozen fryers Nana brought back from the A&P. Scared? Not me! Boy oh boy! I couldn't wait to write Michael about this!

It was only a little after six o'clock in the morning; the ole rooster was blaring away from his perch atop the henhouse. Already I could feel the beginnings of a steamy day. The whole week had been wet and hot, full of mosquitoes and weak winds. The sun and rain had worked their magic on the earth. Grandma's front yard was full of red, yellow, pink, and orange zinnias and red and yellow roses. White and yellow daisies made a trail right in front of the porch. Bumblebees and hummingbirds circled the flowers, then zoomed in for the nectar. The white two-story clapboard house seemed even starker behind such dazzling colors. At the end of the yard where the land started, a full, pretty tree was bursting with tiny hard green balls. I called it the ammo tree, because the little green balls stung when I hit Jimmy and Johnny on their smooth, round heads with them (they always hit me on my bare legs). Behind the house to the side of the barnyard, Grandma's vegetable garden was crammed with little shoots: green beans, butter beans, tomatoes, cucumbers, watermelons, and squash, and the tiny heads of the collards and turnips were just beginning to show. Beyond the vegetable garden on one side were rows and rows of hard, low plants that would soon bloom into cotton. On the other side of the house, going toward the lane, I saw stalks of corn with tiny ears poking out. Near where Daddy parked his car, the pear and fig trees had already flowered and were loaded with fruit. Before I left in August, Grandma would begin preserving and canning the fruits and vegetables that were growing all around her. But today was going to be more exciting than just cooking up some dumb ole pears and figs. Today she was going to kill the chickens. Just as soon as she caught them.

The frenzied chicken skidded on its tiny bird legs, reversed its direction, and headed toward the pigpen. Big Boy, Grandma's fattest hog, lolled in the mud, barely grunting as the hen neared. Grandma plodded behind the chicken. She wasn't walking fast. She wasn't breathing heavily. She just kept coming. The squawking bird, spying Grandma, turned and raced back toward the vegetable garden, almost crashing into Frosty, the white mule, who stood placidly, his eyes flickering as he watched the chase. The rest of the hens, about thirty of them, lined up along the edge of the yard, clucking and observing their sister's misery with growing excitement. Everywhere the chicken went Grandma followed, a little slower, but steady. Finally the bird just seemed to give up. Backed itself up against the fence that bordered the garden. Stood there frozen and terrified as Grandma swept down and plucked it up by its feet.

I was right behind Grandma, so eager for the slaughter to begin that I almost stepped on her heels. I didn't want to miss one bloody minute. This was better than sitting through three monster movies at the Senate. This was gonna be gooood! The bird's body slapped against Grandma's thighs as she trudged several yards to the mountainous pile of wood next to the smokehouse. Grandma slammed the hen down on the chopping block; the bird let out a screech that probably woke up all the Moores lying in the family graveyard way beyond the cotton field. In the same instant,

Grandma came down on the little neck with one lightning swoop of the ax. Whackorooni! The small head hit the ground with a soft thud, landing right at my foot, sprinkling blood on the toe of my white sneakers.

I froze. I stared at the red blood on my white sneakers and had my first conniption right there. I felt the blood dripping down into my shoe and dribbling against my foot, and I jumped into the air so high and so fast that Frosty brayed at the sight. When I came down I was screaming as loudly as the decapitated chicken. Blood! On my leg! Ugh! Ugh! Ugh! I was scared of blood, and the sight of that twitching head dripping blood and guts from its beak and neck was worse than any nightmare I'd ever had. *It was gonna get me!* I dashed around, wild as the headless chicken, looking for safety. Grandma! She'd protect me. I grabbed Grandma Mary's dress and a good hunk of her as well. My grandmother wouldn't let the Headless Chicken get me. As long as I held on to Grandma Mary, I was safe.

As I clung to the folds of her blue dress a hush went over the barnyard. The little head at my feet was motionless. Now the rest of the dismembered bird went into a death dance, wailing and pitching its headless body across the yard, leaving a trail of blood and feathers behind. I was riveted by fear and revulsion, watching the chicken die. Then the Headless Chicken whipped its mortally wounded body around and commenced dancing my way. I raced toward the woodpile. Only I didn't let go of my grandmother, who stolidly held her ground. Not only didn't I manage to get away, I tumbled right into the path of the Headless Chicken. The creature's shrieks pierced the air. So did mine. *"It's gonna get me! It's gonna get me!"* As the bloody hen inched closer I wrapped myself around Grandma Mary's leg and hid my eyes in her flesh. If I was going to be eaten alive and drenched in chicken blood, I didn't necessarily want to see it.

"Get up, baby," Grandma commanded, but I only clung to her more tightly. All I could envision was the Headless Chicken jumping on me and taking my head off. The only safe spot in the world was Grandma's leg, and I wasn't moving.

"Get up, now. It's done gone."

There wasn't a sound in the whole barnyard. I lifted my head just a little and managed one tiny peek. I didn't see the chicken.

"There it is yonder," Grandma said.

I turned my head around. Dragging itself to the center of the yard, the Headless Chicken was in the last stages of collapse. Several of the hens that had stood back to watch suddenly rushed forward, pecking at the body.

"Ugh! Ugh! Ugh!" I said.

"Shooo-ooo!" Grandma shouted, and the chickens scattered like dust in a windstorm.

"Shooo-ooo!" A little distance had made me bold and bodacious. I imitated my grandmother, chasing the hens to the far corner of the yard. The Headless Chicken lay in a bloody heap in the center of the yard. It wasn't moving.

"You loves your chicken fried or baked?" Grandma asked me after she beheaded the three chickens, carried them back to the house, and plunged each one into a pot of boiling water to loosen up the feathers. We were sitting on the back porch. The air still carried the odor of scalded flesh. Grandma was in a hard-backed chair, her two front feet caked with dust and stretched open to a wide V in front of her. Rhythmically she pulled handfuls of feathers out of the chickens' bodies and threw them into a big paper bag on the floor by her feet.

"Fried. Both."

"Which, Miss Lady?"

"Fried the best."

"Okay. Grandmamma gone fry you some chicken."

 Rowing in Amboy

I.

Out beyond this particular point of land far enough you can see the beginning of the curve — periplum — and imagine how all this once made a paradise, deer walking down to the waterside, lapping quietly at the base of trees where the fresh water pooled after the tide pulled out, and turning their overlarge heads now and then at the splash of a wave.

Otters dove for clams in the old bay, making their own wake. Sunlight, spring, and summer heat nourished multiplicities of plants. Small animals chewed at the roots, birds pecked at seeds. Nothing vast had occurred here for thirty million years, all this land sloping gently toward the water. To the west a river flowed out of very old hills, but here it bled away into marshes before lapsing into the bay.

On the old sand, horseshoe crabs, looking like catchers' mitts on legs, walked sidewise toward each other to do battle or mate, and past the spit of land ran big schools of small fish. Imagine the peace, a million years at least of only animal noise and thunderstorms, the wind in the branches, the boom and crack and lightning hiss of rain above the trees, the wash of waves in winter winds, the snap and crash of ice in the coldest part of winter.

For a thousand years this point of land showed no special beauty, only the tranquility of its own solitude. From earthworm to owl, from roots to treetops, it held a pleasure all its own. It was young and it was ancient, it was spare and yet a miracle of spectacle in miniature in the plentitude of small creation: this particular point of land that had no name because no one lived here to speak one.

2.

I don't know how it would have been, born into a town without a coastline. A river alone would have done, I suppose. Plenty of people live interesting lives growing up alongside rivers. But the beach, and the bay leading out into the great ocean, these elements to me made all the difference.

The ebb and flow of waters, the detritus, flotsam, treasures left behind on the sand, the marine life, fresh water and salt mingling in the tides, the sound of buoys on summer nights, bells, horns, the ships anchored within sight of our playlands: the hope this gives you as a child, there is almost no explaining.

3.

So on this particular afternoon I was the one in the stern, navigator, tourist, witness, yet still carried along on the adventure. The sky seemed all one perfect piece of light blue glass, without a cloud to mar its smooth and slightly glowing surface. Turn the world upside down and look up on it and you would have sworn that it was a bowl of glass blown by the master of the craft, no flaw, no streaks, not even an imperfect ray of reflected light, a bowl into which all of us might have slipped and slid, rolling to the bottom where we would have been prisoners forever since without sprouting wings we never could have scaled the sides to the lip and freedom.

But here we were, rowing on the bay whose waters were tufted with little white tops when a breeze blew up now and then but which remained for the most part calm, almost a lake where we boys could have our fun without the threat of deeper trouble that the ocean signified. The pull of the tide did not seem strong, not that we paid much attention to the surge of the tide, either coming in or going out. It was just a small rowboat, a simple outing for us, and tide was something that only seagoing sailors had to worry about.

Here was the layout of our little pond: on the opposite shore from the dock where we started out, the beaches of Staten Island, where we often played. And to the south of us, on the far shore of the river lay South Amboy, with its rails and power lines and blackened wreckage of the piers and jetties that one late afternoon some years before, more than half our lives at that time it seemed, a vast explosion had ripped apart, flesh and wood and stone. Some terrible things had happened that day, and the waves of that explosion still rolled out across the years, though at that time and that place we couldn't know all the shock, all the story, only those parts that had directly touched ourselves. And as for the present, we were rowing! rowing! and tragedies grand or pathetic were things we left behind on shore.

We were rowing! to where the bay widened at the confluence of the Arthur Kill and the Raritan River. Oil tankers and freighters dropped anchor here to wait for tugboats to tow them up the kill under the Outerbridge Crossing and past Outerbridge Reach to the docks at Port Newark or west upriver to the refineries, where their dark holds full of oil would be siphoned off into the huge tank farms that bordered the town just beyond the road bridge to South Amboy. Out beyond the tankers the harbor light stood rooted in rocks in the center of the bay. (I'd heard stories that one magical winter morning early in the century, when my own mother's mother had been only a little girl herself, the water had frozen to a depth so thick that people from town rode their sleighs all the way out to the light. But in this warm weather now, with the current tufted white in the slight wind, that freeze seemed only a dream or a miracle no one would ever wish for!) Beyond the light lay the ocean, Europe, Africa, places we knew only from our geography books and the movies we saw each weekend uptown on Smith Street.

But the tankers anchored before the light were like textbooks in themselves, a catalog of countries and flags, German ships and Nordic ships and Japanese ships and Arab ships and African ships, bearing flags with stars and crescents and animals and scimitars and mountains and clouds and fire and fountains, a field of flags in the air above the slightly undulating waters of the bay. And sailors, seamen of all kinds, in uniform whites and blues and grays and in work clothes of various hues light and dark and sometimes shirtless and sometimes wearing round hats and square caps and smoking cigars and cigarettes and pipes and working on deck or fishing off the stern or swimming off the bow.

Sometimes we'd approach these ships, rowing as close as we could without endangering ourselves with the possibility of a sudden wave heaving us against the side of a vessel or against the huge dark mossy chains that ran from the ship into the water where the anchor had been dropped. Sometimes there'd be no one on deck and we'd row around the entire length of a tanker, watching for activity in the lower portholes or on one of the lower decks. And now and then we'd be rewarded with the sight of a man in a chef's hat peeling vegetables or two or three sailors throwing a ball back and forth or one of those lone fishermen or a few divers. The divers, the swimmers, were the ones we liked best, because now and then they spoke to us in greeting, calling out in their native tongues or once in a while flinging a heavily accented *hello* or *good morning*.

It embarrassed me when my foreign-born father spoke this way in front of my friends, but out here on the water, with these strangers — adventurers, sailors! — talking in their odd accents, the world felt like a story in which I was playing a principal role.

"Hi!" we'd call out to the men.

"Hello!" they'd sometimes call back.

"Hey!" I'd shout. "You there!"

All the while we were rowing to keep ourselves within hailing distance, bobbing up and down in the flow, hoping to keep this tenuous contact with visitors from other shores.

"You like to swim?"

"Oh," a sailor called to us from where he stood leaning out on the anchor chain, his long hair plastered down over his neck like a seal's, "oh, yes! Yes!"

And another would splash up to the anchor chain, grab hold, hoist himself up, and call to us, "You come too? Yah? Yes?"

And we'd laugh and smile and hold up a hand to show that we considered ourselves helpless, capable of rowing out here but not of diving off into the heaving waters.

And then the wind would shift and turn us about and we'd get caught up once more in the business of rowing, and the swimmers would wave to us from the giant anchor chain, and we'd watch them over our shoulders as we pulled back toward shore, until the sailors disappeared against the darkness of the water and the ship itself in sunlight seemed to brighten out as if in flame spreading against the larger sky. And we rowed back to shore and returned to our families in the houses where we lived, on the verge of but not quite yet understanding that land was not solid and houses were like ships and time was like water, like a river feeding into a great salt bay and the ocean beyond, where eventually everything gathered, everything found and lost.

STUART DYBEK

 Thread

The year after I made my first Holy Communion, I joined the Knights of Christ, as did most of the boys in my fourth-grade class. We'd assemble before mass on Sunday mornings in the sunless concrete courtyard between the convent and the side entrance to the sacristy. The nuns' courtyard was private, off-limits, and being allowed to assemble there was a measure of the esteem in which the Knights were held.

Our uniforms consisted of the navy blue suits we'd been required to wear for our first Holy Communion, although several of the boys had already outgrown them over the summer. In our lapels we wore tiny bronze pins of a miniature chalice engraved with a cross, and across our suit coats we fit the broad satin sashes that Sister Mary Barbara, who coached the Knights, would distribute. She had sewn them herself. At our first meeting Sister Mary Barbara instructed us that just as in the days of King Arthur, the responsibility of the Knights was to set an example of Christian gentlemanliness. If ever called upon to do so, each Knight should be ready to make the ultimate sacrifice for his faith. She told us that she had chosen her name in honor of Saint Barbara, a martyr whose father had shut her up in a tower and, when she still refused to deny her Christian faith, killed her. I'd looked up the story of Saint Barbara in *The Lives of the Saints*. After her father had killed her — it didn't say how — he'd been struck by lightning, and so Saint Barbara had become the patron of fireworks and artillery, and the protectress against sudden death.

Our sashes came in varying shades of gold, some worn to a darker luster and a bit threadbare at the edges and others crisp and shining like newly minted coins. We wore them diagonally in the swashbuckling style of the Three Musketeers. It felt as if they should have supported the weight of silver swords ready at our sides.

Once outfitted, we marched out of the courtyard into the sunlight, around St. Roman Church, and through its open massive doors, pausing to dip our fingers in the marble font of holy water and cross ourselves as if saluting our Lord — the bloodied, life-sized Christ crowned with thorns and crucified in the vestibule. Then we continued down the center aisle to the front pews that were reserved for the Knights.

In the ranking order of the mass we weren't quite as elite as the altar boys, who got to dress in actual vestments like the priest, but being a Knight seemed an essential step up the staircase of sanctity. Next would be torchbearer, then altar boy, and beyond that, if one had a vocation, subdeacon, deacon, priest.

Though I couldn't have articulated it, I already understood that nothing was more fundamental to religion than hierarchies. I was sort of a child prodigy when it came to religion, in the way that some kids had a gift for math or were spelling whizzes. Not only did I always know the answer in catechism class, I could anticipate the question. I could quote Scripture and recite most any Bible story upon command. Although I couldn't find my way out of our parish, the map of the spiritual world was inscribed on my consciousness. I could enumerate the twelve choirs of angels. From among the multitude of saints, I could list the various patrons — not just the easy ones like Saint Nicholas, patron of children, or Saint Jude, patron of hopeless cases, but those whom most people didn't even know existed: Saint Brendan the Navigator, patron of sailors and whales; Saint Stanislaus Kostka, patron of broken bones; Saint Anthony of Padua, whose name, Anthony, I would take later when I was confirmed, patron of the poor; Saint

Bonaventure of Potenza, patron of bowel disorders; Saint Fiacre, an Irish hermit, patron of cabdrivers; Saint Alban, patron of torture victims; Saint Dismas, the Good Thief who hung beside Christ, patron of death row inmates; Saint Mary Magdalen, patron of perfume.

I could describe their powers with the same accuracy that kids described the powers of superheroes — Batman and Robin, Green Lantern, the Flash — but I knew the difference between saints and comic book heroes: the saints were real.

I didn't doubt either their existence or their ability to intercede on behalf of the faithful with God. In the dimension of the spiritual world there was the miraculous and the mysterious, but never the impossible. At each mass, we would witness the miraculous in the transubstantiation of bread and wine into the body and blood of Christ. And when I encountered mysteries such as the mystery of the Trinity, I believed. Mystery made perfect sense to me.

My holy medal turning green around my neck, I practiced small rituals: wore a thumbed cross of ashes on my forehead on Ash Wednesday as a reminder of mortality, wore a scapular wool side against the skin of my chest as a reminder of Christ's suffering, and I offered up my own small suffering as I offered up the endless ejaculations I kept careful count of for the poor souls in Purgatory.

That was an era for ceremony, a time before what my aunt Zosha came to derisively refer to as Kumbaya Catholicism, when the mass was still in Latin and on Good Fridays weeping old women in babushkas would walk on their knees up the cold marble aisle to kiss the glass-encased sliver of the True Cross that the priest presented at the altar rail. After each kiss, he would wipe the glass with a special silk kerchief for sanitary purposes.

It was a time of cold war, when each Sunday mass ended with a prayer "for the conversion of Russia," a more severe time when eating meat on Friday, the day of Christ's crucifixion, could send a soul to Hell. Before receiving Communion, one was required to fast from the night before. To receive Communion without fasting was a mortal sin, and there could be no greater blasphemy than to take the body and blood of Christ into one's mouth with mortal sin on the soul. Sometimes at Sunday mass, women, weak from fasting, would faint at church.

Once mass began, the Knights would rise in unison and stand and kneel to the ebb and flow of the ceremony with a fierce attention that should have been accompanied by the rattling of our sabers and spurs against the marble. Our boyish, still unbroken voices were raised in prayer and hymn. At Communion time, it was the privilege of the Knights to be the first to file from the pews, leading the rest of the congregation to the Communion rail. There we would kneel in a long row of navy blue slashed with diagonals of gold, awaiting the priest. Often the priest was Father Fernando, the first Mexican priest at our parish. He'd served as a chaplain in the Marine Corps and lost an eye to shrapnel while administering the last rites to dying soldiers in Korea, and he distributed the Eucharist to us as if reviewing the troops. Usually Father Fernando wore a brown glass eye, but he'd been shattering glass eyes lately — the rumor was he'd been going out drinking with Father Boguslaw — and when he'd break one he'd wear a pair of sunglasses with the lens over the good eye popped out.

Sometimes, approaching the Communion rail, I'd be struck by the sight of my fellow Knights already kneeling, by their frayed cuffs and the various shades of socks and worn soles. It never failed to move me to see my classmates from the perspective of their shoes.

One Sunday, sitting in the pew, watching flashes of spring lightning illuminate the robes of the angels on the stained glass windows, my mind began to drift. I studied my gold sash, upon which the tarnishing imprint of raindrops had dried into vague patterns — it had begun to rain just as we marched in off the street. There was a frayed edge to my sash, and I wrapped a loose thread around my finger and gently tugged. The fabric bunched and the thread continued to unwind until it seemed the entire sash might unravel. I pinched the thread and broke it off, then wound it back around my finger tightly enough to cut off my circulation. When my fingertip turned white, I unwound the thread from my finger and weighed it on my open hand, fitting it along the various lines on my palm. I opened my other palm and held my hands out to test if the balance between them was affected by the weight of the thread. It wasn't. I placed the thread on my tongue and let it rest there, where its weight was more discernible. I half expected a metallic taste of gold, but it tasted starchy, like any other thread. Against the pores of my tongue, I could feel it growing thicker with the saliva that was gathering in my mouth. I swallowed both the saliva and the thread.

Immediately after, when it was already too late, it occurred to me that I had broken my fast.

It would be a mortal sin for me to receive the host. Yet the primary duty of a Knight was to march to the Communion rail leading the congregation. Not only was the enormous humiliation I would feel if I remained seated while the others filed up to the altar more than I was willing to face, but in a sudden panic I worried that I'd be kicked out of the Knights, my ascent up the staircase of sanctity over almost before it had begun. I sat trying to figure a way out of the predicament I'd created, feeling increasingly anxious, a little sick, actually, as if the thread were winding around my stomach. I thought about how not a one of my classmates would have even realized that his fast had been broken by swallowing a thread, and since he wouldn't have realized it was a sin, then it wouldn't have been one. It didn't seem quite fair that my keener understanding made me more culpable. Perhaps a thread didn't count as food, I thought, but I knew I was grasping for excuses — it seemed a dubious distinction to risk one's soul upon. The choir was singing the *Agnus Dei;* Communion would be next. My suit coat felt pasted to my back by a clammy sweat as I thought up various plans at what seemed a feverish pace and rejected them just as feverishly. Maybe I could pretend to be even sicker than I was feeling and run from church with my hand over my mouth as if I were about to vomit; or I could pretend to faint. But not only did the notion of making up a lie in order not to receive Communion seem too devious, I didn't have the nerve to carry off a spectacle like that. To do so would probably be a mortal sin against the Eighth Commandment; I'd just be getting myself in deeper.

Then a detail mentioned in passing by Sister Aurelia back in third grade when we practiced for our first Holy Communion occurred to me. She'd told us that if, at the Communion rail, one should ever realize he had a mortal sin on his soul that he'd somehow forgotten about until that moment, then he was merely to clasp a hand in a *mea culpa* over his heart and bow his head, and the priest would understand and move on.

Communion time arrived, and on trembling legs I marched to the rail with the other Knights. How fervently I wished that I were simply going to receive Communion. I felt alone, separated from the others by my secret, and yet I became aware of an odd kind of excitement bordering on exhilaration at what I was about to do. Father Fernando wearing his one-eyed pair of dark glasses approached, an altar boy at his elbow, holding a paten to catch the host in case it should slip from the priest's hand. I could hear their soles on the carpet as they paused to deliver a host and moved to the next Knight. I could hear Father Fernando muttering the Latin prayer over and over as he deposited a host upon each awaiting tongue. *Corpus domini nostri Jesu Christi . . . May the body of our Lord, Jesus Christ, preserve your soul in everlasting life.*

So this is the aching flush of anticipation, I thought, that a penitent sinner would feel, a murderer, perhaps, or a thief, someone who had committed terrible crimes and found himself at the Communion rail.

Father Fernando paused before me, and I clapped a fist against my heart and bowed my head. He stopped and squinted down at me through the missing lens of his dark glasses, trying to catch my eyes and having a hard time doing it with his single good eye. Finally he shrugged and moved on, wondering, I was sure, what grievous sin I had committed.

I never told him, nor anyone else. I had swallowed a thread. No one but God would ever be the wiser. It was my finest hour as a theologian. Only years later did I realize it would be that moment I'd think back to when I came to wonder how I'd lost my faith.

PATRICIA ELAM

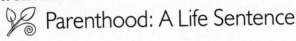 Parenthood: A Life Sentence

My mother, a librarian-turned-housewife, packed healthy lunches with fresh-baked cookies, always tucking in the daily comic strip to make us smile and remind us of her love. My father shared a successful law practice with his brother and another attorney. We couldn't eat dinner until he came home, no matter how hungry we were. We lived in a stately gray house surrounded by a patch of trees in the Roxbury section of Boston. (The city later tore the house down so they could build a park, citing urban renewal.)

Our house was a block away from my grandparents' home, where we went on Sundays after church to feast on my grandmother's spectacular fried chicken and showcase our talents. Grandma commanded performances from her grandchildren. My baby brother Keith chose a Jewish song about a dreidel so many times that even my grandfather knew it by heart. Jay usually portrayed a character from a story he was enamored with, and I'd select a ballet or modern dance. Jocelyn was the baby, so she didn't have to do much beyond gurgle and look cute. Our cousins performed as well; there was never any avoiding it, especially on big holidays like Thanksgiving and Christmas. It got worse when Grandma saw the Supremes on *Ed Sullivan*, because then she'd want us to sing one of their songs and dance like them.

In our household, we had precise and regimented homework time, bath time, reading time, and bedtime. The only thing that distinguished us from the families on *Ozzie and Harriet, Leave It to Beaver,* and *Father Knows Best* (my favorite shows then) was our brown skin, nonexistent then in the world of television programming. Our parents strove to make sure our experiences were well rounded. Although we attended predominantly white schools in pursuit of a strong academic education, at home we were immersed in the knowledge of who we were as black people and the contributions our ancestors made to the world. It was important to our parents that our pediatrician and dentist were black, as well as the other professionals whose services they used. Consequently we came up knowing that the possibilities for black folk were endless, contrary to what some in our society would have had us believe.

⚜

I was the oldest child. Jay was two years younger, Keith was eight. Jocelyn was exactly ten years younger than me. (We lost a sister at three months old. She would have fallen somewhere between Jay and Keith.) When we were small, our mother's enthusiasm often seemed bigger than whatever we had accomplished (a "hip, hip, hooray" for pouring our own juice, a deluge of hugs and kisses for tying our own shoes or writing in cursive). My siblings and I joke that we grew up "victims of *positive* verbal abuse." Don't get me wrong — our mother doled out her fair share of punishments, raised her voice when perturbed, and spanked us when she was even more perturbed. Mrs. Barbara Elam could wield a pretty mean belt or palm of the hand. (Back then, "spare the rod and spoil the child" ruled.) And when she did it, she'd throw in one of those classic guilt-instiller phrases, which never made any sense to me — "This hurts me more than it hurts you" or the one I found most troubling, "Stop crying or I'll really give you something to cry for." Unfortunately, I remember one of those *extremely* rare occasions when it was I who drove her to that point.

At that time Jay and I were the only children born to my parents thus far. He was about five and I was about eight. Earlier in the week I had discovered a beehive in our yard, underneath the back of the house. I suggested to my little brother, who was always eager to please during those days, that he might want to hit the hive with a stick, the same way he'd hit a baseball with a bat. You can guess what happened — but even I was surprised at the horde of furious bees that rushed at my brother. Our mother, aroused by Jay's screams, came outside, scooped him up — vengeful bees in tow — and without hesitation took him inside to the bathroom, closing the door behind them. From the look she flashed me as she carried Jay away I knew she'd be back. And she was — in full effect. She spanked me until my stubborn tears showed up.

Although my mother says she regrets never learning to swim or ride a bike or conquer the latest dances, we pretty much took it for granted that she could do anything. After all, she could cook like a chef, run a meeting, nurse a wound, quell a fear, listen with patience, hem an outfit, sing a lullaby, help with homework, and read the same story over and over, when pleaded with. She never tired of reading to us, because she loved books more than anyone I know. She made it her mission to instill that love in us as well, so we were inundated with books. Every holiday, birthday, and just because. Her love of reading went hand in hand with her disdain for television. The rationing of TV watching was a fine art with her. Jay remembers smugly turning off the television just in time, he thought, only to have his clean getaway dashed when she came in and took the temperature of the boob tube. I don't actually remember my mother watching television when we were little, unless it was the *Hallmark Hall of Fame* or somebody black on *Ed Sullivan*, but I can certainly recall the image of her reading. A comfortable straight-backed chair, ankles crossed, brow furrowed, and lips slightly parted as if in a trance. We'd have to call to her several times to get a response, and we often teased her that the house could have burned down around us while she kept reading, like Nero with his fiddle.

✂

When I was four or five, perhaps, I began dancing on my father's shoes. He and I danced like this at family events, weddings, anniversaries, birthdays — but sometimes we danced in the living room to Ella Fitzgerald or Nat King Cole. I would slide my Mary Janes onto his black tie-up shoes and lean in close to him, holding tight and wrapping one short arm partway around his legs. He'd lower a hand onto my shoulder and clasp my free hand in his, extending it out, tango style. And then we'd dance in one sweeping motion with my shoes glued to his. If my feet slipped off, he'd quickly scoop me back up onto his toes. It was the thrill of a merry-go-round ride or a Ferris wheel as he spun me, rippling my dress and petticoat like an unexpected summer breeze. As the creases in his smooth brown face gathered into a slow smile, he'd laugh from way down low, deep and rich and strong.

My mother told me he wanted a daughter first and couldn't have been more delighted when I came along. He didn't call me his princess, but I knew I was. I have a picture of us, more than thirty-five years old, taken at a community parade. I am dressed up as the Little Old Lady in the Shoe — my father's idea — standing beside the huge "shoe" he created from my tricycle, big cardboard boxes, and poster paint. He stands proudly behind his shoe on wheels; I stand beside it rather nonchalantly, taking for granted my father's hard work, creativity, and energy expenditure.

We grew up knowing that our father worked hard in his law practice and that he was well respected in our community. We heard just how respected every time one of us even thought about doing anything remotely questionable. Wherever we were, all we had to do was state our last name and someone would pipe up, "Are you related to Lawyer Elam?" And later, when he became the first black municipal court judge: "Are you Judge Elam's daughter?" Why did he have to know so many people? we wondered. And why were so many of them police or law enforcement types? Our father was mostly quiet, serious, stern yet patient when confronted with our misdeeds. The times when our father *did* lose his patience were not pleasant, but we all knew it took a lot to get him there.

He was a looming, kinglike presence in our lives. We sought his approval far more than our mother's. Maybe because she was always around. Whatever the reason, we especially wanted him to see the *A*'s on our report cards, notice the rainbows we made from construction paper, watch the way we rode our bikes with no hands. And although we loved having our mother read to us each night, it was a particular treat when Daddy was the one, because he didn't just read. He *performed*, making faces, moving his body and deepening his voice or stretching it to a higher pitch, in accordance with the story's dictates.

On weekends he was home, mowing the lawn, fixing our bikes, and, after church on Sundays, taking us for long drives in the station wagon that embarrassed my brother Keith, who fervently wished he'd trade it in for a Mercedes. But he and my mother decided to educate all four of us in private schools, because the Boston public schools, especially in the black neighborhoods, were in a shambles. So we never did get a Mercedes.

Our parents always presented a united front. There was no running to one after the other had turned us down for something. If one said no, so did the other. They supported, honored, cherished, and worked with each other as equals. Even though our mother's role was in the home with us, my father valued her opinion on big decisions and he helped out around the house. He taught us that real men shop for groceries, vacuum the carpets, and do laundry. And our mother's exuberance was the antidote to my father's cool calm.

As we grew older, our parents tell us, they grew tired. That supposedly explains why Jocelyn got to wear pantyhose at an earlier age than I and why Keith could stay out later than Jay when he was sixteen. And Jay and I often couldn't believe the things our younger siblings got away with saying to our parents — things we were certain would have warranted a spanking or at least a punishment! But for all the comparing we did of which child got which preferred treatment, our parents never compared us. Each of us was an individual in their eyes, and they adjusted their mold of child rearing to accommodate our differences. Education remained of utmost importance, but creativity was also greatly encouraged in our household. Our parents somehow managed to raise four artists.

When I (now a novelist and writing teacher) began writing and illustrating my own books as a little girl, my mother praised them proudly and helped me sew the pages together so that they would resemble real books. When Jay (now a drama professor at Stanford University) dressed like Santa Claus in the midst of August, my parents didn't chastise him. Although he was punished for slicing up his brand-new Easter coat to resemble the pleated waistcoat favored by George Washington, my parents couldn't help admit how clever it was. The early rap scribblings of my brother Keith, a.k.a. Guru, internationally renowned rap artist, had my father a little concerned, but my mother aided him in seeing the poetry in the work, and now my father fashions his own raps for family events and speeches he's called upon to give. My sister, Jocelyn, known for her creative classroom teaching style, wrote poems as a child, created sculpture and paintings that were displayed on every available door, wall, table, and counter space when she was small.

When some of us made adjustments to our careers in order to better pursue our art, our parents were open to this and celebrated our need to be who we are. After all, they are artists as well. My father has written musicals, plays, and songs. Most of my mother's letters are composed of elegant prose and poignant poetry.

Looking back on a childhood I didn't appreciate enough and sometimes was embarrassed by, because I thought it wasn't an "authentically black" experience, I understand now that for many, my childhood scenario is only a fantasy. And even for children who aren't experiencing violence or dire poverty, there are other issues. Large numbers grow up without two parents, and even those who have them rarely sit down at the dinner table anymore. There's no one around to help with homework, because a single parent is working two jobs just to make ends meet. The quality of public education is as poor in many school districts as it was in Boston when my parents made a decision more than thirty years ago to educate all of us in private school. Being a parent is hard work. I have heard people say that all we can do is strive to give our children at least what we got, and with luck, a little better than what we got.

In my case, what I got was the ideal, and I try (often failing miserably) to live up to it on a daily basis. Sometimes I call my parents with desperate queries like "How did you do it? How'd you raise us without sacrificing your sanity?" Mother will usually talk in depth about her child-rearing philosophy, while my father likes to say that having children is a "life sentence." His voice as he says this sounds serious and stern, but I'm certain that if I were looking at him, instead of listening over the phone, his eyes would be smiling back at me.

 A Child's Garden of Verse

Winding down the lane, the old horse cart suddenly broke its wheel and ran off the cliff. Not crashing beneath, but hanging there like a butterfly caught in a spiderweb. Eek! Heidenroeslein screamed, Eek, I'm too young to die! But too late. Above in the shivering sky, the stars made their last appearance to her limpid eyes, which shone like limpid pools. The rocks below unfolded themselves like they were sheets on a bed — just in time as the cart tumbled off the cliff. Down, down to the rocks she fell, lifted now and then in the air like a butterfly wing. But all she could hear were the voices of the rocks: Time to change your life, Heidenroeslein. Time to change.

1968: It was only the third grade, but the spelling words on the test seemed like fifth or even sixth grade (how *appearance* got in there, she'd never know). — *100 percent correct, Omo*, the teacher said brightly, using a shortened version of her name, Omolara: child born at the right time. It was an African name, a regal gift from her parents, who'd fancied themselves so radical, only the girl did not feel regal at all: eight years old and already heavy-hipped, with gawky glasses and brown-blond hair that stretched across her head like a swim cap. Her truest friend was a small, thick-lined notebook in which her life swooned and receded like miserable waves at the beach.

In the third grade, she had only an inkling of where to find her faith.

Poetry (she remembered from long ago) was the only balm:

words that could be shaped into oceans of music on the notebook line. Poetry helped her deal with the real cause of her suffering — her mismatched parents. Just what had they been thinking, getting married and having her and then expecting her to just *be*? The other children in her class, where construction-paper icicles decorated the classroom wall in paltry designs of winter — the other children all thought she was a freak. At least, that was what their parents in the neighborhood said: *White and black don't make a spectacle together. Black don't love white. Black don't marry white. Black and white don't have themselves no kids.* And yet, here she was.

Some days were good days. Her only human friend in the neighborhood, Suleika, came over on good days for "Tea Party" or "Red Light, Green Light" or "Ladies' Legs," and they played until it couldn't be decided whose legs looked most like teacher's or whose could already be in the movies, like Maria's legs in *West Side Story*. Those *love-haunted* legs. When things got around to *West Side Story*, that was when Suleika usually went home, brooding like a volcano, because she wanted to be Maria *all the time*.

The rest of the days were pretty much bad. Parents in the neighborhood glared at her as she walked down the street from the bus stop to her house; kids gave her the finger, called her names (Half-and-Half, Zebra, Oreo); trees refused her shade, and sidewalks slipped out from under her feet. Every now and then there were miraculous things, objects that felt like pieces of stars like bricks trickling from the sky onto her open head. — *Am I dreaming this world*, she would ask herself, in tears.

But at home it was her parents telling her to buck up, to turn the other cheek, to remember that God don't like Ugly. *Utter foolishness.* Most days were like that.

Yesterday, for instance, was a bad day. She had been forced — by her mother — to write a thank-you letter to her grandmother in Germany, despite the fact that she could not write in German, that her grandmother wouldn't know the difference between the words *doll hotel* and *you smell*. A doll hotel was what she had hoped her grandmother would send her from Germany in her Christmas package. Instead she'd received a book. *A book!*

It was in German, a useless language: odd letters and shapes and symbols in a white person's language that echoed to her: *You're Different! You're Different!* German was her mother's language, a tongue fit only for spiced Christmas cookies and Swiss cheese, for hurting and apologizing and hurting some more. At first Omo hated the book, using it as a coaster for her afternoon cup of cocoa; gradually she used its pages to fan herself or to prop up her pillow as she wrote out her spelling words from the workbook.

Once Omo sat at her little girl's desk in her pink frill room in the upstairs of their house and stared at the book. Useless? Can a present wrapped in Christmas paper ever be entirely useless? She removed it from its coasterhood and read

> Sah ein Knab' ein Roeslein stehn,
> Roeslein auf der Heiden
> War so jung und morgenschoen,
> Lief er schnell, es nah zu sehn,
> Sah's mit vielen Freuden.
> Roeslein, Roeslein, Roeslein rot,
> Roeslein auf der Heiden.

Omo choked on her cup — *Oma von Stein!* Why had it taken her so long to realize that these shapes and letters meant that this was a book of *POEMS?*

She couldn't believe her eyes — before this, all she'd ever seen was the school library copy of *A Child's Garden of Verse*, lovely and dusty in its own right, *but this! So many SHAPELY POEMS!*

Omo leaned in closer to study the poems, all of which were adorned by engraved pictures: some had hills, others meadows, creeping vines, cliffs, bosoms, luscious lips, ladies' hats with feathers tucked in them, knickers on grown men. In a fit of anger, her mother had penciled in a rough translation under the German words of the poem on the first page: it was about little rose-girl, who didn't want to get plucked. Omo was moved by the round, engraved face of the rose-girl, which beamed her sorrow like the sun. There was a boy in the poem, who threatened to pluck her despite her thorns like daggers. Despite her words. That miserable boy. The rose-girl's defense was of no avail. She died, according to Omo's mother's pencil.

Foolishness.

(Why couldn't her mother have been born black like the rest of the neighborhood? Why couldn't her grandmother have sent a Christmas package from Africa instead of Germany? Why had her father insisted on a name that only made people laugh instead of feel proud?)

Foolishness.

Omo's mother walked into her bedroom and asked why she was crying. — I don't understand a thing, the girl lied, pointing to the book. — Is it a rose trying to stay alive in the garden, or is it a boy trying to make the flower into . . . *his wife?*

— You'll understand one day, her mother said gently, getting up to open the venetian blinds. Late afternoon poured into the room like orange syrup. — One day, my darling.

But what good was *one day?*

At night, after lullabies and kisses, the girl sat at her desk and opened her third-grade notebook (while her flagrant parents sat downstairs in the living room, drinking glasses of wine and laughing *to themselves*), and she studied the empty pages intensely, understanding that she would have to come up with her own poetry. Her own shapely words, her own logic. Because how could a boy marry a rose? And how could a rose be anything like a lady, with grown legs and heart? Her poetry would solve mysteries like that.

So her pen got to work. Poems like poems and poems like stories. Instead of love, though, she thought about how she wished the world would treat her.

The next day in the classroom, rickety portraits of Martin Luther King (colored in by the first grade) were being pasted on top of the icicles, and Omo sat beaming at her desk. She wore her usual penny loafers and corduroy jumper, but her hair was new: golden brown as the burned dune grass at the bay beach and braided tightly, warrior style. Around her, children practiced writing their names in cranky cursive across the gigantic lines of their notebooks. She, on the other hand, flipped reverently through her pages as if she were consulting a museum's best work.

The teacher walked by all the desks, checking spelling words, math problems. She picked up Omo's notebook, glanced at the words, then put it down. Children turned their heads and waited. They'd always thought of her as a freak.

— You ought to be put in the fourth grade, the teacher said blithely.

And that was all it took. She wouldn't ever need that doll hotel. Stars that fell like bricks would never rain again. Poetry was a balm. The girl had been saved.

Armed with a gun the kind soldiers had used in the World War, the warrior approached the injured woman and sniffed her skin. She was more dead than alive. He put the gun aside and wept. His friend, the warrior Millie, then cut through the rope with her bare teeth and began mouth to mouth resuscitation on the injured woman. The last man — a handsome pastor — grabbed the gun from the warrior and vowed handsome revenge. He took an ice cream from his pocket and began to feed the woman who was too weak to even open her lips and thank them. If she could have spoken, she would have looked into their eyes and said, — Gracias.

1972: The Spanish have moved in at the curling edges of the neighborhood, but they keep to themselves. She wants to be friends with them, with the Spanish girls who are in Special Ed because they can't speak English, and the boys who, fascinated by the waft of her corduroy jumper, raise their eyebrows at her. One day, in a silent corner of her room, she breathlessly recites their names like a litany of saints: Eduardo, Jesus, Milagros. She has seen their nametags at school. She has heard the teacher yelling at the top of her lungs. Omolara dreams of being their Anointed.

Another day her mother makes a lunch of peanut butter and jelly sandwiches and says to Omo, — Stay away from that crowd.

— Why, she asks. — They are friendly. They speak to me. They see me.

— Stick to your own kind, the mother whispers, and again Omo is thrown into confusion. What is her own kind? She says nothing, though, because she knows that the other mothers in the neighborhood tell their girls the very same thing.

Another day Omo rides the school bus home to the neighborhood and is promptly chased down the street by a group of angry girls who've been curious about her since the first grade. Their curiosity has traditionally come out in their fists. As she runs, Omo sees the Spanish kids standing on the sidewalk up ahead. They are eating those delicious sticky coconut ices you can only get at the curling edge of the neighborhood. Omo wishes they would come and save her, but the Spanish kids don't move. They are eating and chatting and laughing and sometimes standing silent. Do they notice her? Do they care? One of the angry girls pins Omo to a dead oak in someone's front yard, and then fists are raised yet again. The Spanish go silent. These angry girls mean business.

Their names are Shelly, Mona, Linda, Rita, Martha, and Frankie (sometimes there are more, and sometimes fewer), and they have long gotten over the fact of Omo's mismatched parents; now it's *her* they don't like, with her fake white girl's hair and her too-short corduroy jumpers and her beautiful ugly eyes and the fact she thinks she's better than the whole lot of them, pretending to be Spanish instead of plain old ugly half-and-half. The angry girls know she has a benevolent fairy grandmother hidden away, someone who sends Christmas packages filled with candies and cookies and poetry books. *Candy and cookies and poetry books — now wouldn't that be nice for a change? Why we don't have a grandmother like that?* They pin her tighter against the dead oak (Rita's mother, Mrs. Sanders, looks out her window, drying a casserole dish in her hand) and they threaten to gouge her eyes. — *Why you look at me in school like that? Why you cross your eyes? You saying I'm that ugly? Huh? Is that it, you white-black stuck-up?*

She recognizes Suleika in this pack. — You used to love me, Omo whispers to her.

Suleika blushes, then twists a piece of Omo's fleshy arm between her fingers. — Don't remind me of those days, she mumbles.

Mrs. Sanders then dashes out of the house waving the casserole dish like *she* means business, asking the angry girls why do they have to be such bullies, and why can't they leave the poor wretch in peace, and so on and so forth. The girls walk away, kicking up the neighborhood dust with their patent leather toes, vowing to kick some bona fide butt one of these days. Omo turns and looks across the way at where the Spanish kids had been standing, but now there are only wisps of smoke in place of the children. There is the smell of coconut, the taste of asphalt, the feel of impending brick shower in the air. — *Did I dream them,* Omo wonders, rubbing her eyes. — *Will that always be me?*

She goes home and flops on her bed and cries. Closes the venetian blinds. Peels off her jumper, socks, and underwear and blows air from her mouth onto her naked stomach. Takes out from under her pillow her grandmother's most recent letter (*I missing you, You missing me, Yours Truly, Oma von Stein*) and rips it to shreds. Opens her seventh-grade notebook and studies the story.

It is a fairy tale that has no beginning and no end. Omo feels she has always written it, and will always continue to write it, until she is as mysterious as her own grandmother, steeped in hills of lebkuchen and marzipan and shapely alphabets: a fairy tale concerning the life of Eduardo, who has nighttime arms like a tree

1974: And there she is, her German grandmother, Oma von Stein, live in the flesh, standing in their living room, admiring her mother's drapes. Handmade, just like everything else in the house. Hand-sewn upholstery, antimacassars, throw pillows. Christmas tree ornaments stitched out of satin and felt. Hand-dipped candles on the Advent wreath. Even the rug is handmade — a hooked rug, similar to the kind Omo's father's mother makes out of empty bread-loaf bags (only unlike Oma von Stein, Omo's father's mother lives down South, in a house full of dogs and cats, and sends up her yearly Christmas present to Omo in a thin envelope: a five-dollar bill and a card that reads, *Happy Birthday to Jesus*).

Her German grandmother looks different than Omo had imagined: a youngish face, gray eyes, legs that could beat Maria's any day, and a voice that patters like rain. She smells of a cologne that is worn every day, not just on special occasions. And she is full of wild love, wanting to hug her granddaughter from sunup to sundown. — *Can you love me without words?* is what her arms seem to demand.

Oma von Stein sits down with Omo at homework and sighs over the math problems the girl is scribbling out, mysterious equations and frightening symbols. — *In my day*, Oma von Stein says, but only because that is one of the few phrases she has been able to master; smiling at Omo, petting the girl's rough brown-blond head as if she were a favorite kitty.

In her day there was only simple addition and subtraction. Nothing complicated like what's in front of them.

Then, after supper, as she and Omo are washing and drying dishes, Oma von Stein asks, in English: *Who that boy?* She is, of course, talking about Matthew, the white boy in school who has a crush on Omo and who leaves roses in their mailbox every afternoon. Omo's mother finds him quaint, and always recalls the days when she first met Omo's father. What gloriously romantic days, those. (*Humph*, Oma von Stein will grunt. Those days are not a good memory for her.)

— *Who that boy?*

— He's just a friend, Oma. I know him from school.

— *You love? Lieben?*

— He's a friend.

— He look *Jude*. To me he look *Jude*.

And Omo learns that that word means *Jew*, and she begins to bite her nails whenever she sees Matthew in the hallway at school. In truth, he is her best friend. But she is weak; she makes excuses in the school hallway, then dashes home from the school bus before her German grandmother wakes up from her nap and buries herself in homework, just so that later she won't have to look up from the book or table. When she is alone, Omo scribbles his name in the shape of a wreath along the margins of her notebook. But then she finds the roses before anyone else does, and throws them straight in the ash can.

It is days, then weeks without any hint of Matthew. Her mother laughs and asks, — What's the matter now? *Aren't you two in love anymore?*

— *What do you know*, Omo replies under her breath.

Outside on the street, the angry girls stare at her with her lovely white grandmother, out for a walk in the middle of the day. They don't do any chasing anymore. Their eyes are filled with something else. One of them, Rita, is taking German 3 in school. Shelly is learning how to sew drapes in home economics.

Suleika stops by one evening with bad news: her own grandmother, the one who also lives in the South like Omo's father's mother, has just passed. There are tears in Suleika's eyes.

— I'm sorry, Omo says. Though in her heart she is rejoicing.

> One soup bone,
> one armful of turnip greens,
> one dash of nutmeg,
> one mixing bowl full of flour,

> *one potful of simmering rice,*
> *one cupful of sugar, one handful of yams,*
> *all souls of desire.*

1975: Surprisingly, several neighbor ladies come to the house (dressed in feather hats and white stockings as if they were on their way to the Baptist Tabernacle), and they bring sweet potato pies, corncobs covered in foil, Dutch ovens full of rice and peas, aluminum pans dripping with spareribs. Omolara is not used to this kind of food, nor is she used to this kind of hospitality: wasn't it *that* neighbor lady who used to call her mother (now dead a week) white trash? And wasn't *that* other neighbor lady the very same person who used to spit on the sidewalk right in front of their house, asking in a loud voice why God had robbed them of *yet another good black man*? None of these ladies ever appreciated the fact of her parents. But what can they say now, since her mother lies dead in the cemetery over on Harrison Avenue? Lung cancer. The disappearing dust of a mother in the earth. Omolara studies the ladies who now sit in her living room, handling some of her mother's embroidered antimacassars, breathing in the stale air of the house, crying as they touch her father's tear-wrinkled hand. She longs to touch them, to see if they feel like her mother.

The neighbor ladies continue to come, day after day: fried chicken and turnip greens and loaves of Wonder Bread and jars of peanut butter. Her father is so beside himself with grief, he forgets he even has a daughter, and so the neighbor ladies start to fuss over her. *Why, this head hasn't been combed in a week, seems! Look at her clothes, we got us a regular Little Orphan Annie on our hands! Girl, your mama is in Heaven and she'll never forget you.*

But Omo has to make sure. She takes out her tenth-grade notebook and starts a series of little scribbled poems about ocean waves, how they just keep on hitting the shore and pulling back again and hitting the shore again in devastating monotony. Suddenly she tosses the notebook under her bed and covers her eyes. She knows she should have listened better.

When her mother had said the word *cancer.* When her mother called from her hospital bed to make sure Omo had completed every stitch of her homework. When her mother breathed her last breath in the loneliness of the night. When her mother appeared to her in a dream and told her to do the right thing. (Why hadn't Omo invented a prayer to God, instead of relying on the old safety of poems in the notebook?)

Her penmanship had become sloppy. There were no more rhymes left in her. Every day now, miraculous stars like bricks fell on her head and made her near unconscious. No memories other than this ridiculous ocean. Why remember an ocean? They lived only a mile away from the bay, and Lord knows the waves at the bay were just childish things. Nothing like the ocean.

Notebooks are foolishness, she concludes under the blur of spent eyes.

I'll do anything for you
I'll climb the highest mountain
I'll swim the largest sea
But only if you promise
You have to come back to me

1977: At the burger stand, sitting in the back seat of the car, chewing her nails into infinity, Omo remembers a poem she'd written way back in third grade. Those were good days. Magnificent days. Now gone forever. With one hand, she rubs the creases of the corduroy wales that lie against her belly — this is what the neighbor ladies call being *in trouble.*

The poem she'd written back then had been about buildings and flowers and the simple act of kindness. How good it had made her feel. But now. Poetry is a crock when put in the wrong hands. This boy who used to be her best friend but now is something else — Matthew — this boy writes poems that sound like Mack trucks. He would be the best replacement for her mother if only he could let his mind soar off cliffs and into rose patches. If only he could write something real.

He has been hers, though, for some time: Matthew, with his pearly skin, chocolate eyes, walnut nose, excellent comradeship. He would be the best replacement. His poems, though, are wordy, trite, and lovey-dovey; they are worse than cancer.

Omo sits in the parking lot, ravaging her fingers to the bone. Matthew thinks she needs to be eating *more healthier things*, so now, at the burger stand, he goes in to order burgers and chocolate shakes and onion rings, things he thinks she would like. He says to her, — Now wait right here. I'll *make* you happy.

All she wants, however, is the meat of her fingers and the keratin of her nails. Her mouth always tastes of eggs these days, and that is a horrible taste. So Omo makes plans. She'll refuse everything. She'll walk out of the car and straight into the waves at the beach. She'll meet her mother under water, a mermaid splashing with the starfish instead of an earthly pile of disappearing dust.

But no, she won't do any of that. She'll eat those burgers and fries. She'll listen to the rest of his Led Zepellin cassette tape. She'll agree to blow-dry her hair. He is about to become her husband, and so she must obey.

There was no question in his mind when she first told him. — We'll get married, he said, — and give it a good home. A name.

— My mother would've killed me, she admitted. — If she'd lived.

— Love conquers all, replied Matthew (who fancied himself a poet after taking that Regents English class).

— But what JOB do you have, she asked, — and when are we supposed to GRADUATE from HIGH SCHOOL?

— I love you, he answered, with bewilderment on his face. — I love you. *Doesn't that mean a thing?*

In trouble. She has not told her father, because she knows that thirty-seven is too young to take seventeen. Besides, he still is in a fog of grief. The comforting neighbor ladies still come around, but they don't know the truth either. They can't smell the baby on her yet. They are too busy forcing their daughters to make friends with this poor girl (no more of this terrorizing the poor mixed wretch who can't help it if her parents were black and white *back when* they weren't supposed to be). The girls aren't angry anymore, only indifferent, and perhaps that's more hurtful. Mona comes by daily, held up by the scruff of her neck. Rita also comes by, asking what it is like to have a real German grandmother, and then starts to cry for no good reason.

Time passes slow as syrup, but the formerly angry girls don't notice a thing. Little by little, they all choke themselves on a mixture of pity and relief that they believe to be the equivalent of friendship. Omo knows better.

— *You not half bad*, Mona said one day in the shade of the dead oak tree.

— *You kinda funny*, Shelly admitted, next.

— *When your mama was alive, I bet she used to laugh at all your stories*, said Rita later on, sitting upon Omo's mother's last reupholstered chair.

— *Your mama probably used to love those poems you wrote there*, said Linda, up in Omo's room, flipping through her pages.

But Omo was not moved. *Why pretend to love me?* she asked them in her mind. *All those years of chasing, all those years of running. Could I help it if Africa wasn't ever a place in your hearts?*

Martha came by to visit as summer drew to a close. She brought Frankie along, and together the girls eyed Omo suspiciously. Her aroma was becoming clear to them, frightening. — *Damn, Omolara*, Martha said. — *You looking awful strange these days. We bet your mama wouldn't like the way you looking.*

— *And how's that?*

— *Well*, said Martha smugly, — *if it was my mama, I wouldn't be in your shoes like that.*

And Omo started laughing, thinking to herself, *Your mothers are made of the same disappearing dust as mine. One day it'll be your turn.*

Now in the car, she closes her eyes as the bag of french fries is opened and dreams of Suleika. Her truest friend, truer than the notebook these days. Yesterday they lay together on Omo's frill bed watching the leaves on the trees from her bedroom window; most had already turned into a frozen red mold in the branches. As Suleika talked, Omo was wondering what her German grandmother would be sending this year for Christmas. It had been a long while since Oma von Stein's last letter. She had come for the funeral, had had words with Omo's father, then disappeared.

— You got yourself in trouble, Suleika was saying.

— Well, this proves that my legs are more like Maria's than yours!

And the girls laughed. (Later on, when she relates this to Matthew, he won't get the joke. He'll be leading her down the aisle at Town Hall. His father is the justice of the peace there, and he asks the kids to be quiet. Town Hall is no place for whispers.)

Snow has completely covered the windshield. Omo stops chewing her fingers and looks down at the piece of paper Matthew scribbled to her just that afternoon: a poem, something to make her heart sing. But it does not have that effect. Lovey-dovey, trite. Full of leftover roses and girls who turn to dust. And Omo cries as if the heavens were caving in that very minute. *Her* mother had wanted her to write poems for the ages. *Her* mother had wanted her to go on to college. *Her* mother had wanted Omo to savor love as if it were candy on the tongue. So many foolish things.

— *Get yourself taken care of*, Suleika had whispered yesterday on the bed. A friendly, sweet whisper. Not like old times, but then just like them.

— Taken care of? How?

— *There are places for girls to get it done for free. Early and late.*

— Look at where I was! Look at where I am!

— *Don't cry, Omo. Don't cry. I personally know of one over in Elm Beach.*

❧

Be kind to children
Be kind to flowers
Be kind to people and buildings and towers
Living is fun
For a year and a day
Be kind to me
And hear what I say:
THANK YOU!
THANK YOU VERY MUCH!

1966: A soft October day, when she was arguing with her first-grade teacher over the spelling of one word on her test. There was a *p* and an *i* and a *z* in it, so naturally the word had to be *pizza*.

— No, the teacher said wearily. — But Omo, you are almost there.

She was absolutely positive — in that little girl's way — that the grown-up world found immense joy at her dazzling display of intelligence, her seeping creativity. Only last week she'd dictated a story to her mother, a story containing all the spelling words from that week's test:

Car
Corn
Dog
Pen
Whistle
Door

And her mother had laughed at the story, saying *Brilliant, baby, brilliant!* and hugging her daughter like wildfire.

— Don't ever leave me, the mother had whispered during their embrace.

— I won't, Omolara had replied. But that was back when there was no darkness ahead. Last week. The tunnels had been well lit.

The teacher cleared her throat. — What's the word, then, Omolara?

The girl hugged her thick-lined notebook against her chest.

She felt her mother's eyes on her even though her mother was no-where nearby, was at home most likely, rolling out dough and se-cretly smoking cigarettes. Omo knew the word on the list was *pizza* — why couldn't her teacher admit that? *Such foolishness.*

In another corner of the classroom, the girls from her neigh-borhood played "Miss Mary Mack" and didn't ask her to join in. She couldn't yet figure out why. But she listened anyway — those words had such lovely rhythm and rhyme.

The teacher asked, — Why not try sounding things out, Omolara?

The girl would not give up. She closed her eyes.

— Give someone else a turn then, the teacher said, and it was right then that Omo was hit by SPELLING LIGHTNING and blurted out the real word: *prize.*

— Very good, Omo. Very, very good.

When she told her mother about it later (over an auburn set-ting sun, and the sounds of the neighborhood rosebushes embrac-ing each other, and the wisps of Parliament 100s spiraling in the air), her mother clapped her hands and said, — I knew you'd get it, baby. *I knew it in my heart.*

Because Omolara, she was never one to give up.

MERRILL JOAN GERBER

 from *The Kingdom of Brooklyn*

Polio lives, a wide green bug with blinking red eyes. It hides beneath the iron grates of the drinking fountains at the park, in the silver sprinklers of wading pools, on the rims of cups in restaurants, on the headrests at the movie theater. If you inhale deeply, it can ride into your lungs on a single breath, splash up from the toilet at school, enter your nose if you lean down to smell a rose. No form of "be careful" has ever been like this, no warning to watch out for cars, for wild dogs, for bad boys, for bullies has ever had this edge of hysteria to it.

No. No. No. Not only is "no" the twenty-four-hour song in *my* ears, but the Skaters hear it, the Girl Scouts hear it, the listeners to radio hear it. *"No"* is affixed to the sky above us like skywriting. No wind blurs or blows it away.

Esther Tempkin, a fellow Girl Scout whose father is a doctor, distributes special cotton masks at our Girl Scout meeting and warns us to wear them if we have to go on the subway, the trolley, or into crowded waiting rooms at the dentist's or doctor's office. Her father has seen "terrible cases," she warns us — at the first sign of a sore throat or a stiff neck, we must rush to the doctor. She waggles her tongue in her mouth and rolls her eyes in her head to show what it will be like if we don't take care. She's a beautiful girl: red-haired and luscious-looking, though not a tramp at all (the Bike-Riders and I have discussed this). She has "developed" but wears loose blouses and big sweaters. She has been the first in our troop to see blood — we regard her as a successful warrior queen. She has seen blood and she has survived.

After her demonstration about how we are to wear the cotton masks, she invites us all to her house Tuesday night to watch *The Milton Berle Show*.

"Isn't that going into a crowd?" a Scout asks.

"People you are with regularly are not a threat," Esther says, quoting her father. "It's strangers! Watch out for strangers!"

Television, though we have all seen it, still seems a miracle. Milton Berle is a legend — a man who wears a dress and lipstick. Esther Tempkin has told us that at her house they have placed a magnifier over the screen to make the picture bigger. I know what that means: Dr. Tempkin is rich — all doctors are rich.

My mother says she could have married a doctor. She tells this to my father when they are arguing about whether or not I can go to Esther's house. My father thinks I should not go: the doctor has his office in the downstairs of the house — and is not a doctor's office the most dangerous place to go? But my mother says a doctor knows what precautions to take. She wants me to see what a doctor's house is like. She wants me to keep these matters in mind when it's time for me to marry.

She also reminds my father she could have married a lawyer. Before she met my father, when she worked as a legal secretary in Manhattan, she met "all kinds of important men who wanted to marry me." I don't know what she expects him to do when she says these things to him. What can he do? He isn't a doctor. He isn't a lawyer. Perhaps she is saying these things for my benefit: If she had married a doctor, then *I* would have a television. If she had married a doctor, then *I* would be the one giving out cotton masks and have special information to protect my friends from the red-eyed glare of the polio bug.

We are sitting on the new rattan furniture when my mother

makes her "could have married a doctor" speech. I now think of the talks with my father as speeches, because the two of them don't exchange words; she lectures, he listens.

The Screamer has other matters to attend to. She's much bigger now, the Screamer/my sister, with her straight, neat hair, always with her head down over some jigsaw puzzle or follow-the-dot book, or coloring book, or cutout book. She's of no interest to me. I ignore her, or I blame her if I can, or I mess up her dolls-of-foreign-lands collection — I do whatever I can to make it hard for her. I would be happier without her, but she's here forever. I am trying to learn not to spend all my time trying to understand why what's here forever is here, or what's gone forever is gone — just as I don't think, if I can help it, about my grandmother. There are just certain rules that are permanent. You can't cry or whine to change them, you can't kick or hit, you can't beg or plead, you can't sulk or vomit. The things that won't change sit there like a brick wall: they don't hear you, they don't move, they don't go away, they don't change.

But my mother and father *do* change. Could they also go away? From each other? From me?

My mother has a new hairdo; though Gilda knows every style and how to make it, my mother announced that she was going to a beauty shop on Avenue P to have it done: an upsweep, with many hairpins to hold the hair, swirled into a roll, against her scalp. Without hair around her face, loose and white, she looks narrow and thin; her skin looks tight, as if hairpins are also holding it stretched. Her mouth stretches over her big, unreal teeth. She has new clothes now, too — I don't remember much about her old clothes, but the new ones are silky and fancy, pale gray with weeping willows imprinted on them, or white, with the silhouettes of black panthers standing out. She wears high heels and nylons these days, because the decorator who came to do the house wore high heels and told my mother her legs would look good in them.

I have to be careful with the rattan furniture; if I am nervous and pull at the splinters that stick out, I can bring the whole couch down to the floor. I am warned. My mother warns me every day. So instead of picking at the splinters, I pick at the dry skin of my lips. If I peel off one layer of my delicate flesh, very slowly, my lips turn red. They look as if they have lipstick on them. The main problem is drinking orange juice. Then my lips burn as if I am dipping them into liquid fire.

"I want Issa to see what a doctor's house has in it," my mother says. "I want her to see what kind of furniture they have, what kind of dishes they have, what kind of silverware they have. She has a right to know what's out there in the world."

My father, smoking his pipe, picks at rattan splinters at the edge of his chair. His curly dark hair has gone a little flat, and his thick, strong fingers are flat out on his thighs. My father seems flattened. It's strange, but there seems to be less of him, although he hasn't gotten thinner or smaller.

He works as hard as ever: longer hours, more days. The antique store is open on Saturdays now. And he goes on calls to buy new antiques every night. The women at our house no longer worry at the window that — because he is late — someone has tried to rob him or murder him. There *are* no women anymore to stand at the window and watch for his car to pull up at the curb. My sister is busy with her puzzles and dolls, my mother is busy with her furniture catalogs and clothing magazines, Gilda is alone upstairs, and my grandmother is not at any window anywhere. Even I myself no longer worry about my father now. Some things can't be influenced, no matter what I do.

"So *let* her go to see Milton Berle, *let* her go to see a doctor's house," my father says. He picks up the newspaper. My mother picks up her fashion magazine. My sister moves her bride doll and her bridegroom doll into position on the living room floor for yet another of their wedding ceremonies.

Some of the Girl Scouts in my troop know by heart the opening song of *The Milton Berle Show*, sung by the men who come out on-stage in mechanics' uniforms. They sing along with them:

> We are the men of Texaco
> We work from Maine to Mexico . . .

I settle back against the soft cushions of the couch. So: *this* is a doctor's house. It isn't so fancy. The medical examining rooms are downstairs, and Dr. Tempkin and his family live upstairs. He has a side door in the alley just like Gilda's, with a side stoop and a separate doorbell. It's true that in the center of his front garden — where, at our house, we have only a lilac tree — the doctor has a mirrored ball resting on a tall marble pillar. *That's* fancy. But after all, his patients need to know how to find his house. That mirrored ball must shine very brightly in the sunshine. The sickest person in the world, rushing along Ocean Parkway in pain, would see the rainbow beams fired off that mirrored ball.

I try to observe the doctor's house the way my mother would look at it. Our Girl Scout troop members are sprawled on the furniture in a way that would not please my mother — but Mrs. Tempkin seems not to mind. Esther is a beautiful hostess, wearing a flower barrette in her brilliant red hair, wearing a flowered apron, helping her mother pass around trays of brownies and special paper cups full of malted milkshakes. In the dimness of the kitchen lurks the famous doctor; he is short, bald, with glasses. His name is Dr. Ruby Tempkin. He has the name of a jewel.

I am grateful for the luxury of the paper cups: they are for safety from the polio germ.

Mrs. Gargano, one of our leaders, tells us not to be shocked if Milton Berle comes out onstage wearing a dress. "Men do that for a joke, you know," she says, and we all laugh nervously. My father would never wear a dress, not for a joke, not for any reason. I think of all the fathers of my friends that I know: they would not wear dresses either. (But I am eager to wear boys' clothes. I already do, when I put on my dungarees. They have the zipper on the side, because no girl would wear pants with a fly, but from a distance they do look like boys' pants. They look tough. They look handsome.)

And suddenly there he is, the famous Milton Berle, with a dress, lipstick, a curly wig, a cigar — what an imbecile. Everyone is laughing. I don't think it's funny, really — I think it's stupid. I look around at the lit-up faces of my friends, my clubmates and my Girl Scout buddies. We are all watching a little round screen through a sheet of magnifying glass; we are all watching the figure of a man dressed like a woman, with his hairy legs showing, dancing around.

There's a sense of comfort in being in a big friendly crowd of people I know, a sense of safety and good cheer, but it also feels flat and unreal to me; something inside me withdraws, backs up like a turtle pulling deep into his shell; I can almost feel my skin telescoping like a turtle's neck. I go back to a place in my mind that is deeply familiar and most comfortable: to thoughts of the pile of books beside my bed I wish I were reading, to thoughts about my mother's new hairdo and what it means, to thoughts about Izzy and how I can't wait to see him again, and to thoughts about my grandmother, knotted in the trap of her wet sheets, helpless . . .

But laughter from the world recalls me; I force my turtle-head out of its shell. Reluctantly, I come back to the doctor's living room, I come back to Milton Berle telling a joke and pursing his lips, I come back to my milkshake, my brownie, to the vision of the little clump of blue flowers on the barrette in Esther's red hair.

As we are leaving, I see Mrs. Tempkin pursing her lips against Esther's forehead, a gesture I think is strange. *She's* not going anywhere, this is her home, why kiss her goodbye?

The rest of us circle about in a commotion of leaving, saying thank you, waving to one another, accepting an extra brownie to take home. As we go out into the night, I see the mirrored ball reflecting the moon, big and brilliant as the sun. And from behind it, or under it, or over it — it's hard to tell which — the mirror throws off dull bits of starlight, like chips of broken glass.

My mother wants me to look at what they have here, and so I do. It's true, we have no starry night in silvered glass at our house, we have nothing of this kind at all.

Two days later our troop leader calls to say that Esther is in an iron lung, a cocoon that breathes for her. That the fever and stiff neck struck her the night we saw Milton Berle, that her legs were paralyzed within a few hours. That she can't breathe by herself and can't move. That if we still have the brownie that was given to us to take home, we must flush it away.

My mother's voice when she sets down the phone is pure quivering panic. Not sympathy. Just fury and panic.

Without asking permission, without telling her where I'm going, I dash out front with my bicycle and ride down East 4th Street to the playground. The vast concrete city is deserted, because children are forbidden to come here. I have the entire place to myself. I walk my bike from place to place, examining the silver spout of the drinking fountain, the seesaws (where strangers play), the monkey bars (where strangers climb), and even the spigots of the wading pool, though no spray is coming from them; the pool is dry.

I am looking for the enemy: the wide green bug with blinking red eyes.

An old woman in a black cape, carrying shopping bags from the shops on Avenue P, comes walking through the playground very slowly. She doesn't know me, I am sure, but she walks right toward me. Her ankles are thick, her shoes are heavy and black, laced tight. She has a black babushka tied under her chin. She comes right toward me as if she were supposed to meet me here, and she says to me, "I have something for you." She takes an object tied on a string from around her neck and she comes right up to me and places the circle over my head like a necklace. The thing tied to the string smells like mothballs. My eyes burn as the fumes rise up.

"Wear it," she says. "Don't take it off till the winter. And go home from this place."

I ride home as fast as I can. I am shaking and my teeth are chattering. When I get in the door, my mother is holding the phone away from her body. She looks wild, almost insane.

"Esther is dead," she says to me. "And with a doctor right there."

 Saturday Days

Saturdays Mommy, Gary, and I dusted the entire house then walked to the grocery store then put everything away then sat at the table (which was neither dining room nor kitchen just a yellow table in between) and had lunch. We always played "What I Am Eating" and I always had "roast tom turkey" which I must have thought sounded terribly elegant and sophisticated. Usually there was a tearjerker on television and we would watch Joan Crawford or Bette Davis or Lana Turner and cry and cry and cry. In Cincinnati at my parents' home I always liked Saturday days but Saturday nights Daddy would holler at Mommy autumn, winter, and spring. I couldn't wait for summer because we went to Knoxville to visit our grandparents.

Directly across from 400 Mulvaney there was Cal Johnson Park. It should have been Dr. Cal Johnson Park because Dr. Johnson, a black man, had purchased this land and willed it to the city for the use of black children in perpetuity. It stands yet. There was a creek in the back where our tennis balls could be forever lost and if you cut through the park you could reach Vine Street in half the time without having to climb the Mulvaney Street hill. Grandmother and I saw the Silas Green Revue there, which had to be one of their last shows. In this age of segregation the swimming pool for black kids was in Mechanicsville but we at CJP had the swings.

One of the least-known aspects of my personality is that I am dutiful. Anything I have to do I do and do as cheerfully as I can. But I have to admit I actually like housekeeping. There is something about order that brings peace and comfort. On Knoxville Saturdays Grandpapa would go to the market. This is most likely because Grandmother was both very pretty and very mouthy. She took no prisoners. Grandpapa already knew not to let Louvenia near anyone or anything that would upset her. If, for example, Grandmother had gone to the market, one of the white guys would probably say something totally out of line. Grandmother would verbally abuse him then come home and tell Grandpapa. Grandpapa would be honor bound to go back up to the Gay Street Market and ask for an apology. Most likely that would not be forthcoming so Grandpapa would be forced to shoot the man. The word would spread in both communities that John Brown Watson had shot Mr. White So and So and the black community would hunker down while the white community would liquor up and come dark the whites would swarm down on Mulvaney Street baying for the blood of Grandpapa who would be lynched, the house burned down, and all sorts of various sadness would be visited upon black Knoxville before the Tennessee militia was called out to enforce the peace. The great thing about my grandpapa is not only that he was smart but he could see the logical end to most endeavors, so Grandpapa went to the market and Grandmother and I stayed home to clean.

I'm still not sure what it is about living rooms that makes black women crazy. Every Saturday you dust and dust that room wiping the plastic covering the furniture and since we did not have a vacuum cleaner running the mechanical broom over the carpet. Grandmother didn't change the beds until Monday but we brought out the Old English polish for the furniture and the silver polish for the tea set and I always liked the Bruce's wax in a can for the floors. It's not, by the way, that I like mice because I don't have any particular affection for mice but since we lived in a small town there was always the chance a mouse would get in so Grandmother kept a trap set. I still don't think anything should be in a trap so I hit on the idea of waxing the pantry floor. I was thinking if the mice smelled the wax they would know someone lived there and go on. I don't know what the mice thought but in all my years of living with my grandparents we only caught one mouse . . . and I like to think he was already sick. I not only like housekeeping I am quick. I put my head down and got it done. Grandmother would always go behind you to make sure it had been done right but what she never knew is that I can't stand to be corrected so I always do my very best to get whatever it is right. I did. So I got to go swinging.

I've always thought swinging should be an Olympic sport. I knew, in fact, when synchronized swimming became a "sport" that double dutch would be next. I admire double dutch. Those ropes would pop and the girls would turn faster and faster and the girls running in and jumping out would dance a dance that would make ballet dancers weep from envy. They would jump up and twirl and pass each other on one foot then flip to their hands then flip back up and I would stand amazed. I have no sense of rhythm. All my rhythm is in my head. But I could swing. Swinging took courage and patience and balance and the most difficult maneuver is the dismount. I grew up with iron swings that were set in concrete; none of those recycled things for me. The swing was hard black rubber connected to links of iron. These were swings to take you to the moon. The object, for those who do not swing, was to stand in the seat and pump up. You pumped up as high as you could go. You were actually trying to reach parity with the top bar. When you got "even with the bars" (to which I ascribed 10 points) you "kicked out and sat down in the seat" (10 points). If you missed the seat you could still hold on but it looked really ragged. You then pumped once or twice more to show control (10 points) then (and this was the final crucial ending) you "bailed out." You got 20 points for a perfect landing. If you fell or tumbled over you lost points accordingly. Sort of like a poor girl's parallel bars. The dismount was everything! And I would practice and practice. Pump and jump; pump and jump. Then Grandmother would call me to lunch. But I was ready. I knew I was ready. I was prepared to go for the gold medal. All I needed was a chance.

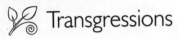 Transgressions

The way of the transgressor is hard.

This I know because I often had to stay after school to write these words in painful script. My teacher in both the fifth and sixth grades, Miss Cain, seemed to think that the force of the lesson would be diminished by anything less than perfect penmanship. No matter how I labored, my writing wavered, my lines were crooked, my letters were misshapen — transgression upon transgression.

Miss Cain seemed to have been born to detect and punish transgressions. She was a small, neat person with a sharp nose, a clenched mouth, and iron-gray hair that was trained into tight coils. Everything that came naturally to me and my classmates — talking, laughing, daydreaming — she found not only distasteful but sinful. I suppose she saw herself engaged in a losing battle to save us from the scorching fires of Hell, but I know that I preferred the style of the other fifth-grade teacher, Miss Melton, who gave us dancing lessons once a week. After lunch we'd gather in the school auditorium, both girls and boys, and Miss Melton would put "The Skater's Waltz" on the record player. Then she'd glide around by herself, showing us the steps, until she chose a partner, a boy to clasp to her large, powdery bosom.

Were those my choices? Was the world divided between the Miss Cains and the Miss Meltons, the transgressors and the waltzers? Of course I didn't really put the question like that, not at that age, but I could certainly see that these teachers, and all grownups, operated in accordance with impossibly complicated rules. And I could see that the world they had created was full of dangers and divisions. Sometimes I think that my chief goal as a child was to steer clear of grownups and their strange convictions.

I grew up in the South. I wasn't born there and left when I was thirteen, but I will always think of myself as a southerner. Or, since my father was from New York and my mother from Pennsylvania, as a southern Yankee. My family was Jewish and Catholic and we went to Pennsylvania every summer, where we still owned a small blue house, but I am from Brewton, Alabama. No doubt the fact that we never really fit in, that we were always outsiders in Brewton, heightened my apprehension of the place and helped sink its hooks deep into my memory and imagination.

I was a toddler when we moved to Alabama shortly after World War II, and one of my earliest memories is of attending mass in the Escambia County Courthouse. This empty part of south Alabama was mission country, and there was not yet a Catholic church. The priest, Father Horgan, was straight from Ireland and spoke in a rich, thrilling, nearly incomprehensible brogue, even when he spoke in Latin. In the courthouse, he set up the altar on a plain wooden table. The congregation knelt on the bare floor in a room furnished with folding chairs and brass spittoons. This was the very room, my father told me, where the Ku Klux Klan had met the night before.

Of course I believed him, though I know now that he was stretching a point. It suited him to dramatize our situation, conveying to his children — eventually there were eight of us — a sense of daring in the practice of our religion. He particularly liked to describe how the ancient Christians, under fear of persecution and death, had worshipped in underground catacombs. He'd been to Rome. He'd seen the catacombs.

So Rome and the catacombs and Ireland had to be factored into my scheme of things, along with chewing tobacco and the Ku Klux Klan, though I never saw a Klansman in a white sheet. Nevertheless, I was absorbing the lesson that the world had been and always would be structured along the lines of serious conflict, and I was one solemn little altar boy, learning the Latin responses so that I could take part in the mysterious ritual that was performed not only at the courthouse but occasionally in our house, too, on the sideboard in the dining room.

Father Horgan was our holy man. On Sunday mornings he drove a circuit from one town to another, traveling in a black Ford whose trunk was full of the tools of his trade — the shiny vestments, his chalice, the Communion wafers, and a small tabernacle fitted with brass doors and surmounted by an iron crucifix. I revered him, though it puzzled me that he was subject to the same afflictions as ordinary mortals. The shoulders of his black jacket were always dusted with dandruff, and he used Scotch tape to hold the gauze pads on his neck. He had a problem with boils.

He'd been uprooted and dislodged, but so had we. We'd moved to Alabama because my grandfather, a textile manufacturer, was looking to relocate his mills in a place where he could cut his operating costs. His name was Horace Levy, and he was a sweetheart of a man who loved the New York Yankees, the songs of Jimmy Durante, and the movies of Abbott and Costello. As a child I equated his Jewishness with his affection for vaudeville and New York City, where we went every summer to visit his sisters, Winnie and Jewel, and ate foods — tongue, gefilte fish, brisket — that were never served in Alabama. I had no grasp at all of the chain of events that had driven him first to Pennsylvania, where he met and married my Pennsylvania Dutch grandmother, and then to Alabama, where he named one of his mills after me. Stephen Spinners was the dye plant. Here the narrow fabrics — heavy ribbons, mostly, used for seam binding and hemming — were brought to be finished. They arrived in large, loose coils, hanging from wooden battens that were placed on a wooden contraption like a mill wheel. As it revolved, the ribbon was dipped repeatedly in the dye vat. The fumes were powerful and scalding. After they'd taken their color, the ribbons were left to dry on large metal racks, then spun onto spools by black women who spoke and sang over the clatter of machinery. Their hands moved at blur speed, and I couldn't understand a word they said.

My father worked for my grandfather, and they disliked one another, but I can say this for both of them: they were fair, and they imparted to me a sense of respect for the people who worked at the mills, every one of them. It wasn't until later that I learned how my grandfather had defied local custom by hiring so many black workers, but I most certainly got the message that I was not to speak slightingly of them or interfere with their work.

This was the South of the 1950s, the separate-but-equal South, and there were rules within rules. Too many of them, frankly, and the local rules didn't always line up with the rules of our household. Some of my school friends said *nigger*, a word that was banned in our household. Nevertheless, I was aware of the high tension when one of the black women who worked for us, Iva Lee, decided that she wanted to attend mass. By that time our church had been built, and Iva Lee and her family showed up in their Sunday clothes. This was surely one of the first times that black and white people worshiped together in Brewton, and I still carry the image of that solemn family at church, an image that was fixed in memory because the occasion felt so momentous.

I have to add that Iva Lee did not become a Catholic, and in fact stopped working for us suddenly. She was a drinker, and one day she simply announced that she was leaving and never came back. The circumstances of her departure were not clear to me then, but I knew that as much as we prided ourselves on our open-mindedness and efforts to be fair, there was a great gap between our lives and those of the black people with whom we came in contact.

There was Ruth, for instance, who took care of me and my brothers and sisters and liked to scare the bejesus out of us. What was she thinking when she took it upon herself to cure my mumps with sardine oil? I was seven or eight years old, lying quietly in my bed, when she came into the room with a bottle and spoon. "This sardine oil," she told me, "will keep your nuts from dropping."

And then there was Lamar, the one-legged janitor at the elementary school, who liked to mess with our minds. "Everyone have eat some shit," he'd tell us kids when we had to stay after school and he got a few of us alone. If we argued, he grew agitated and threatening and came up with ingenious scenarios to illustrate the many ways in which this shit eating could have occurred.

Where did grownups get these ideas? When you got right down to it, there wasn't really all that much difference between the punitive attitude of Miss Cain and the spooky ramblings of Lamar and the teachings of Father Horgan, who told me that my soul was like milk in a bottle, all white until contaminated with sin, which was black, and while a venial sin only tainted the milk, a mortal sin turned it all black as coal. How was a kid to make sense of all this?

I couldn't. No one could, really, and perhaps it is not fair to lump all the grownups together. Yet they did seem — all of them, black or white, male or female, priest or janitor, parent or teacher — to be driven by necessities that even to my child's mind seemed like distortions.

Now, decades later, they still seem like distortions, and I think I can make out more clearly the way that the distortions are wrapped around fears and lies and hatred and intolerance. My real education has been mostly a process of trying to squeeze out, drop by drop, the lessons that so many adults taught me — not maliciously, I know, but because they believed that they had my best interests at heart. Nobody ever deliberately taught me to hate, or to fear, or to lie, or to be intolerant, but those messages were coded into every lesson that set people apart and above one another — whites above blacks, Catholics above Protestants, Yankees above southerners, rich above poor, and so forth and so on forever and ever.

My real education, in other words, has been the effort to recover the purity of heart and mind in which all those invidious grown-up distinctions are once again as bizarre and meaningless as they were to me as a child.

 The Spiral Staircase

What more delicious to a ten-year-old girl than a movie about a mute young girl threatened by a serial killer, only we didn't call them that back then. I could identify, because while no one I knew of was trying to kill me, I often felt speechless, mute and vulnerable. The movie starring the forever innocent Dorothy McGuire, with the whispery voice when she could speak, was set in the wicked Victorian past, not the current, tranquil (it seemed at the time) Paris, Texas. The *Dallas Morning News* critic had said this was a must-see movie.

There were two movie houses in town. One specialized in the ever-popular bloodless westerns and the other in dramas and scary movies. The only film I ever walked out of was in that same scary movie house. *The Strangler.* Not because it was so scary, but because it was so boring. Now *Snow White, that* was scary; all those trees reaching for poor Snow White terrorized me so that my mother had to pull me out in the middle of the movie, way before the prince arrived . . .

The Spiral Staircase was the only movie I remember wanting to see so badly that it led to a screaming fit. I was a fifth-grader. My mother had never objected to my seeing a movie before. Maybe she was thinking of the trauma of having to pull me out of *Snow White.* Or maybe she had realized by then that I generally operated on emotional overload and might freak out. But her refusal seemed stunning and irrational. Crying and flailing about, I argued with her, but her only explanation was that old faithful, "I just don't think it's a good idea." My repeated "why," which usually moved the conversation along to some logical explanation, didn't work. This particular argument stopped there, ending with "Why don't you go play with your new neighbor."

"She's not new," I muttered. The new neighbor being one June Booth, a blond ten-year-old who with her mother, Louise, had been living next door in a furnished rental room for a couple of months. They'd arrived one rainy night in a Yellow Cab with their few belongings. My mother and I, and the other assorted extended members of the family who lived with us then, ran to the window, because we weren't accustomed to people arriving at night or in one of the town's three cabs. The scene seemed mysterious and fascinating, especially since her mother carried a guitar case.

Housing was scarce in those days. We lived three generations strong in our house while also renting out a makeshift apartment. Paris, Texas, had suffered a demographic swell a while back when an army base was set up outside town, bringing strange young men who didn't talk like we did. Sometimes Louise, who worked at Kress, claimed she couldn't even understand them. The changes brought new subject matter and alarms from many pulpits. And June and I had both been awed by photos on dressers or hidden in drawers of what had been considered good Baptist girls with soldiers in nightclubs, the girls dressed in shiny dresses and wearing pompadour hairstyles held together with combs or ninety-nine bobby pins. Bobby pins were big then. June Booth and I were tantalized by such girls, who wore fire engine lipstick and mooned around listening to Frank Sinatra records and singing along with "I'll Be Loving You Always." June and I agreed that going to a nightclub was really our ultimate goal, even over being super Christians.

June and Louise rented from our neighbor Mrs. Love, whose life revolved around a fifteen-pound striped yellow cat named Shrimpy. Mrs. Love would twice a day spread the broad Shrimpy across her ample lap to feed him boiled liver by hand.

The day my mother turned oppositional I headed for June's apartment, pausing in the doorway of her kitchen to watch the Shrimpy feeding scene before heading upstairs. June's mother, Louise, not only clerked at Kress dime store but also wrote country music. Their room, like all of ours, was wallpapered, hers with large cabbage roses on vines. It had twelve-foot ceilings, a metal bed, and what my grandmother called a chifforobe, plus a space heater and a basin. In this room June and I would sometimes lie on the bed staring at the ceiling stain shaped like the state of Texas. We thought that was a miracle with a secret meaning we would one day discover. Unfortunately, a tornado came through the area one month and the stain grew to encompass not only Texas but Oklahoma and Arkansas as well.

The Booths had kitchen privileges, meaning they could keep orange juice and milk in the refrigerator and make toast or cereal or some such modest meal. That was a step above just a rented room. June's mother washed their clothes in the bathtub down the hall, which she shared with Mrs. Love and Shrimpy, who could balance on the side of the toilet to do his business.

June was sitting on the bed working on math. June was a whiz in math, though in her other subjects she was poor, because, I realize now, June couldn't read. She could read songbooks if her mother had already sung the songs, but straight-out fifth-grade textbooks were hard for her. Sometimes I'd read an assignment aloud to her. Her mother didn't get home from Kress until after six, and sometimes June and I would take one of her mother's songbooks and sing along after I'd read the words through. On a few lucky occasions her mother would sing with us.

June Booth was shy, with limp blond hair and a prominent forehead over which she each day curled her bangs with bobby pins as soon as she got home from school. She wore Tangee lipstick, which my group thought shouldn't be worn until you were twelve. Each morning as she studied herself in the dresser mirror, rolling her thin lips to distribute the Tangee, she dabbed her mother's Evening in Paris cologne behind her ears. Since June was mostly silent, our walking to school each day was usually one long unrehearsed monologue from me. Only sometimes June reported on her mother's music business and what song she'd sent to Nashville that week. Sometimes June would sing one of her mother's compositions — mostly about love and betrayal — in a strong country soprano that always seemed surprising coming from the shy, thin girl beside me. Listening to June's strong country soprano, I felt there could be something about June Booth that I hadn't yet understood.

June was in my fifth-grade class at J. G. Wooten Elementary School. At that point, as today and probably forever, girls were socially categorized by their clothing. My friends and I wore print dresses, sometimes made of feed sacks, with puffy sleeves, full skirts, and sashes that tied in the back, and sometimes ankle bracelets. Girls weren't allowed to wear jeans to public school then. The difference in me and my friends with June was that while we each day came to school in a clean, ironed, and different change of clothing, oftentimes June wore the same sash-tied dress two or three days in a row. June's failure to change clothes daily set her in a different social level, but I didn't realize that at the time. Though I did know the bottom of the social rung was poor Irma, who wore the same dress sometimes for a week and who sometimes smelled like sour milk, so that boys would sometimes hold their noses as they passed her.

I introduced June to my five major friends and thought it was only a matter of time before June would become a member of our group. We called ourselves the good-time girls, having no idea there was another connotation. But June never seemed inclined to collapse into giggles as we so often did, or flirt with boys or pass secrets. June seemed to prefer to stand back and watch us with her droopy eyes.

Shortly after the movie crisis I decided that if I gave a party for June my friends would have to accept her into our group. I was also thinking how many stars that would add to my crown for such a Christian deed. So one Monday afternoon I ran up the stairs toward the sound of Patsy Montana on the radio and announced that Mama and I wanted to have a birthday party for her on Saturday.

June was on the floor painting her nails glittery silver, since her mother got a discount at Kress. She held the bottle of polish between her bony knees. June was the only girl in our class who painted her nails.

June lifted her nailbrush daintily and studied me a minute. "Why?" she asked.

"Saturday's your birthday, isn't it?"

She nodded slowly and asked how I knew.

She'd told me she'd been born on the date Hitler had marched into Poland, so I looked that up. We didn't have much, but we always had encyclopedias in their proper dusty place and a daily *Dallas Morning News* and a regular exchange of library books.

"I'll get Mama to make that angel food cake with the fruit in the middle."

June turned back to her nails. Patsy was singing she wanted to be a cowboy's sweetheart. I quickly fell into excitement mode, making the party sound like it would be an assemblage of princesses at a ball.

"We'll get Joyce and all the girls to come." Joyce, the fascinating true leader of our group, was a blonde with naturally curly hair who seemed to do everything right.

I explained how I was going to ask everyone to bring their movie-star scrapbooks and we could climb the pecan tree and slide down the roof of the old coal bin and play swinging statues and maybe explore the Tidwells' house, which had burned down a month ago. "We might find a treasure." It never occurred to me for one minute that June might be thinking of eventualities I was oblivious to. She adjusted one of her pin curls, which for a moment required her to cross her blue eyes, which matched her barrette.

"Well, okay, if Mama says it's okay." I noticed the date already circled in red on the Bluebonnet Rex Cleaner calendar tacked by the door.

"Maybe your mama will sing," I said.

"She'll be working," June replied. "Double shift on Saturday," she added as she waved her silver-tipped fingers up to dry before blowing on them.

That week I handed out invitations with a pink bear beating on a drum. When the day arrived it was overcast, with the sun occasionally showing itself long enough to give hope for a sunny day. My mother had been cleaning and straightening up and doing things Mama said she'd meant to do for ages. She then made the angel food cake with fruit in the middle, with pink icing and eleven candles. She'd also bought discounted candy corn left over from Halloween. The girls were expected at two. Since there wasn't a man around to turn the crank for freezer ice cream, Mama and I walked to town and splurged on Cabell's striped chocolate, vanilla, and strawberry ice cream.

June appeared at the back door at exactly two o'clock, though I'd told her to come early if she wanted to. She was wearing a new red print dress. It had a lace collar; she wore matching barrettes and a sales tag still hanging from the sleeve. After I'd showed her the cake and paper plates and napkins on the dining table and told her I'd dusted and swept the front porch, we went outside and inspected the still blooming red spider lilies. They fascinated us, maybe because of the name or just the fact that we believed the blooms looked like tentacles that might pull us in and swallow us up if we touched them. After that we settled at the piano and played "Chopsticks" until my mother came to the door and rolled her eyes. Then I serenaded June with "Blue Moon." But June got involved with one of Mother's *Ladies' Home Journal*s and wouldn't join in, so we finally went out back and pretended to smoke grapevine, though I kept running in and out to see if anyone had arrived.

By 2:30 Mama said maybe I should phone the girls. I phoned Joyce first, who wasn't at home, then Sonya, who said she was so sorry, she had completely forgotten and now her cousin was there and she couldn't come because they were going with her mother to Penney's to shop. I urged her to join the party, not mentioning that no one was there, telling her to bring her cousin, but Sonya hung up before I could beg or bribe. My other three calls were as fruitless. Two of them had gone to the movies, and one call wasn't answered.

I put the phone down and paused long enough for the situation to sink in. Out the window I could see June waiting for me and holding a grapevine like a cigarette. It hadn't for a moment occurred to me that my friends wouldn't come. Never in my life had I heard of a party where no one came.

I moved to what was usually the warm, safe kitchen and hung on the counter.

"So what did they say?" Mama, wearing one of her Sunday dresses with her thick dark hair all pulled into a bun, was sitting at the kitchen table working on her Sunday school lesson.

Feeling a summary would give it an aura of finality and even greater embarrassment, I gave an individual report, implying that it wasn't their fault at all, just a strange coincidence, but I at the same time imagined each girl with BETRAYAL stamped across her face. Then to my horror I heard my voice quiver. That's when my mother jumped on her horse and took charge.

June had by then abandoned her grapevine cigarette and was now swinging on the tire hanging from the pecan tree in back of the house. The skimpy skirt of her red print dress streamed behind her as we watched her skinny legs pump higher and higher, as if she might just pump herself all the way to a nightclub heaven where girls didn't hurt one another. Then Mama called to her to come in since it was nearly three o'clock, so why don't we move along with the party.

At the cake ceremony June took a long time to make a wish and then wouldn't tell it, but she finally blew out all eleven candles at once. Just as June was poised to cut the cake, Mama said, "And then maybe you girls can go to the movies. June, would you like that?"

On the front porch we ate large slices of cake with the striped ice cream. Mine I ate separately, but June let her ice cream sit on her cake until it seeped into the inner fruit.

"Well, what movie would you like to see, June?" Mama said, smiling.

June grinned with ice cream in her teeth and, as Mama left to retrieve the local weekly, said she'd only seen two movies in her whole life.

"Well, there's Roy Rogers at the State . . ."

"And what else," I asked, knowing full well what was still showing at the Grand. "*The Spiral Staircase*," Mama read, not smiling.

"That's supposed to be really scary," June said.

My mother waited, watching for June's decision. I waited, it seemed forever, as long as I could stand it, praying that June would make the right choice. Then I let go involuntarily.

"*The Spiral Staircase* might be fun," I said, as if the subject had never before been mentioned. My sentence stilled the air and fell like a brick.

I turned away quickly, but not before I saw my mother's expression. I dropped my spoon on the floor. When I'd retrieved the spoon it was as silent as I thought a courtroom would be. Then I looked at June, who was looking at me, and I did the brave thing and looked at my mother, who was no doubt realizing that I was as capable of betrayal as the other girls. I was guilty of a manipulative act and at that moment and for a while I felt as capable of being a criminal as the lawyer my mother had always dreamed of. I could just see numbers of the stars on my crown flickering to dark. Finally June licked the last dregs of ice cream from her bowl.

"I'm sorry nobody came," I said to her.

"That's okay," she said. "I wasn't much figuring on it."

A few minutes later June and I moved down the steps past the spider lilies toward town, where we circled the square once before stopping at the Grand. In those days people went to a movie whenever. If it was in the middle of the movie, you'd just stay to see the first of it. When we sat down with our Cracker Jacks, George Brent was about to strangle Dorothy McGuire, but Ethel Barrymore shoots him and Dorothy McGuire manages to call for help. It wasn't nearly as scary as *Snow White*.

ANTHONY GROOMS

 Christmas, Alabama, 1962

This afternoon, I watched on the television, for at least twenty times, the image of the World Trade towers crumbling. It was the first anniversary of the terrorist attacks that killed over three thousand, and a national day of mourning. Almost every channel had some September 11–related programming. On some channels pundits or politicians debated this or that consequence of the attacks, on others reporters profiled victims and their families. These human interest stories, as they are called, I found more interesting, and more than once tears welled in my eyes and I felt choked. I was sorry for the victims and their families. I was sorry for what they had lost, and afraid; but for the grace of God, there go I. (My sister rode in a taxi through Wall Street not fifteen minutes before the first plane struck.) Still, I wondered, what was my mourning about? It was not grief, after all, for grief is predicated on intimacy, and no three-minute profile on television could ever substitute for intimacy. And though you might say I was intimate with my country, I have a bad habit of putting disasters into rankings. This one, as horrific as it was, couldn't have been worse in terms of human suffering than the Indian earthquake just a few months earlier, or the Rwandan genocide, or any of the world wars. For these I was sorry also. But I did not grieve. I did not mourn. For these, too, I was afraid, and horrified, and fascinated. What is wrong with my heart, I was thinking, that I have drawn a border between sympathy and grief?

Later in the evening, after taking a short telephone call from my wife, who was traveling for business, and reading a brief letter from our son, who is in college, I began again to contemplate the meaning of grief. It came to me that as grief grows from intimacy, it, ironically, also grows from happiness. Yes, I suppose there are many ways to grieve and many things to grieve for, but meditating on it, my most acute grief comes from one particular memory, a memory of a happy Christmas, the last Christmas spent with my mother.

It was 1962. We lived in Titusville, then as now a middle-class black community in Birmingham, Alabama. I was thirteen and Josie, my sister, was seven. We had Bingo, an adorable mutt, which sometimes passed as a Border collie. On Sunday mornings we could have been the models for the picture so often found on church fans of the idealized "Negro" family, smiling brown faces and neat good hair. The father in these pictures, hat in hand, was never as tall as my own, though like mine, he wore the thin mustache on the ridge of his lip. The mother, with her netted pillbox and red lipstick, was never as pretty as my own, but somehow always sturdier, always shapelier.

For my family, Christmas arrived some weeks before the actual day. Its harbinger was as regular as any sign of seasonal change. Some weekday in November, for no announced reason, Josie and I would find our parents dressed and headed out for the evening. We knew, as if they put off a scent, that they were going Christmas shopping. My mother always dressed to go downtown. She wore a suit to work at the Booker T. Washington Insurance Company, the largest Negro — as we had been taught to say — insurance company in Alabama. For shopping, she wore a dress, and at Christmas, she decorated her coat with a holly or snowflake brooch. That year she wore the holly. It was twin enameled leaves, green, with gold trim and red berries where they joined. It shone like neon against her brown wool coat. It seemed to cry out to us, "Deck the halls with boughs of holly — fa-la-la-la-la, la-la la la!"

The sight of it was enough to make us children want to cheer. But we played their game and saved the cheering until after the car had left the yard and its engine droned around the corner.

Another sign. Mother put on the Christmas albums. There seemed to be an anticipatory buildup in the way she planned the selections, beginning with children's music: "Rudolph the Red-Nosed Reindeer," "Frosty the Snowman," and Burl Ives singing "You'd better not cry / You'd better be good / Santa Claus is coming to town." Nearer the holiday, usually after we were in bed, she put on Nat King Cole. My father was crazy for jazz music, and Nat King Cole was one of his favorites, but even he said she played it too loudly. Ah, poor, poor Daddy. She was playing it for Josie and me, not for him. And to me, beneath the covers in my back bedroom, that crooning filled the house like the smell of baking — Nat's soft, resonant singing: "Chestnuts roasting on an open fire / Jack Frost nipping at your nose." On the holiday itself she played the religious carols.

On the Saturday before Christmas we went to see Santa Claus at one of the downtown department stores. At age thirteen, I didn't believe in Santa Claus; nor did Josie, at age seven. I stood aside and watched as she indulged our mother. Josie sat on Santa's bright polyester lap, which billowed around her slight frame like a pillow. Though the lap seemed to swallow her, she posed in such a way as to give the impression that she barely touched Santa, hovering over his lap, ready to spring away at any moment. The gloved, rouged, shiny-bearded white man gave her a halfhearted "Ho-ho" — she was perhaps the twentieth child he had ho-hoed since we had arrived and waited in line, white and Negro together, and the line was only then beginning to get long.

For Josie and me, there was another Christmas ritual — the ritual of the search. Sometime before, we had realized that when our parents dressed to go Christmas shopping, they were not always shopping. Occasionally they went to parties, or to dinner, as Mother had a December birthday. We never saw them bring any-

thing home, unless it was groceries or presents for other people —
gifts they showed to us so we would know what we were giving to
relatives. We knew, in fact, that most of the Christmas shopping
had been done long before Christmas, and the presents were hidden in the house — so when we heard the car go around the corner, like Blackbeard and Bluebeard, we began to search out Santa's
booty. I looked in the high places — above the bureau, on the top
linen closet shelf. Josie, small in size, looked in the cramped low
places — under the beds, at the bottom of the closets.

Exploring a suspicious bag was a delicate undertaking. First
the bag had to be carefully observed, its orientation noted as if
we were archeologists digging a votive from the jungle mud at
Angkor Wat. Was it square to the corner? Or angled just so?
How was it nestled among shoes? A pump casually leaning against
the Parizzi logo could be as telltale as a wax seal. We even noted
the dust. Mother had been known to lightly dust a bag or box with
talcum, so whatever grave thieves there might be would leave
prints.

Satisfied that we could reposition the bag, we moved it carefully, trying not to upset its contents, and teased it open, again
careful to look for tape or string, or even a hair pasted onto it. For
a while *Secret Agent Man* had been a favorite television program.
What little surgeons we were! Lacking forceps and clamps, we
pried into the innards of the bag, noting and describing and taking delight in its contents. That year I found watches. "Oh! A
Timex — it must be for me. And look, another with a pink band
— it's yours — and this blouse and these socks." The larger items,
the telescope and cook stove, were hidden in the attic; locked, the
key on my father's chain.

Our parents played the game as cleverly as we did. First they
feigned ignorance that there was any game playing at all. "Bag?
What bag in the closet? What were you doing in my closet anyway, you little snoop?" Still, they hid the bags where we could find
them, and they knew when we had made our discoveries and de-

liberately set about a campaign of obfuscation. A few days after our discovery, my father, sitting at the breakfast table, stretched his arms over his head, yawned dramatically, and said, "I wish I knew what time it was. But my poor children can't tell time, can they?"

"Oh yes we can," Josie offered defensively, realizing the trap too late.

"But you'll need a watch — a good one like a . . . I don't know — what's a good watch, Claire?"

Mother looked up from the pot of grits she was stirring. "Timex? Isn't Timex a good brand?" Even with her back to us and her frame bent with exaggerated intent over the pot, I could see she fought to keep from bursting with laughter. And then sometime halfway through breakfast, she and my father, at last, broke.

"What is so funny?" I shouted, exasperated. I knew the joke was on us children. They only laughed harder. Mother tried to placate Josie's frustration with a pat on the head, but her laughter intensified and knotted until she could barely breathe.

As it turned out, when we saw those watches again, they were on the wrists of our cousins, having been intended for them all along, and left as decoys.

For Christmas Eve supper, our father fried a pan of oysters. It was a custom he had brought with him from Virginia, where he had extended family, and where he had been in college at Hampton Institute. Oysters weren't the only things he cooked, but they were the best. He bought them already shelled, and as he emptied the containers of mollusks into a colander to drain them of their gelatinous liquid, he talked about the times he and friends collected them from the pilings of bridges and piers at low tide, broke open the shells with pocket knives, and let the plump, sandy flesh slide down their throats. He demonstrated by eating one from the colander. Mother shook her shoulders with disgust. She forbade

Josie to follow suit, but that year she allowed me the pleasure, and when I wanted to spit out the gritty lump, she wouldn't let me. She held my head against her breasts, my ear pressed against her heartbeat and her laughter, and made me swallow.

The cooked oysters were quite a different kind of pleasure. Breaded and fried in bacon fat until crispy and seasoned with bits of bacon, they were served with fried potatoes and onions. Mother cooked biscuits, and for something green — collards.

After supper Daddy had his Christmas drink, Jim Beam on the rocks. He put Josie on his lap, and I sat on the arm of the chair while he read "The Night Before Christmas," stopping after each verse to take a sip of the bourbon. I loved the smell of it on his breath.

Then we watched television. It was aimless viewing, the killing of time, until Josie and I heard the weatherman report seeing Santa Claus on radar. He said that the air force radar had picked up an unidentified blip near the North Pole. A second bulletin told us it was headed in a "southerly direction" across the tundra of Canada. Even for the adults, such news caused momentary agitation in case that blip should turn out to be a Soviet missile. Earlier that year Father had brought home a booklet on how to build a bomb shelter in the basement. Our home had no basement, our yard no storm cellar. Finally we adopted the notion that in spite of its steel industry, Birmingham was not an important target. Washington and New York would be blown up first. By the time the Russians got around to targeting Birmingham, we would be halfway to Grandma Pic's, my mother's mother, who lived in the country.

The weatherman, a rather rumpy fellow by the archetypal name of Bubba Jones, announced that it was an unidentified flying object, yes, one pulled by eight tiny reindeer. Now came the time to leave out cookies and milk for Santa. Of course we tested the treats to make sure the milk was fresh and the cookies sweet and crunchy. "We wouldn't want to give old Saint Nick a bellyache."

Father poured a bourbon for Santa, and a second one for himself. Then for a time the house was noisy, our energy perked by sugar and anticipation, but soon after came the long fight against drowsiness. Our parents never made us go to bed early on Christmas Eve — what was the use? We watched television, we listened to music, we danced, we read stories, we told stories, and we laughed. But eventually Master Sleep won — and long before the eleven o'clock report on the unidentified blip, which bore down on the Magic City with all the rapidity and uncertainty that each tomorrow brings.

As often, I awoke early on Christmas and sneaked past my parents' bedroom to peek under the tree. The tree had been left alit, its branches coated with artificial snow, aluminum icicles, and angel hair. It glittered so, it seemed to spin. Underneath, the presents were, as if by magic, already out of their boxes and assembled. That last good Christmas morning, when first I saw the telescope, my breath caught on the back of my throat. It was beautiful: a white cardboard tube angled toward the ceiling and standing on three wooden legs. The Edmonds Scientific Company logo was positioned just so. A montage of sixth-grade science lessons and NASA liftoffs and scenes from sci-fi movies flashed through my head. But it was not yet time for the Christmas gifts. We children had to wait until we were awakened. Even if we had been awake for hours, we knew to lie in our beds and wait for the parents. The ever-increasing anticipation was excruciating, and I believe Mother planned it just so. It seemed that when not only our hearts but our bladders were about to burst, we would hear the first stirrings from our parents' bedroom. First their low voices, and occasional chuckling. Then the squeak of the bed as they moved to the edge. Mother kept her robe at the foot of the bed, so she would be putting it on as she stood. Daddy did not wear a robe, even though he owned one or two. Strap undershirt and boxers

on, he headed to the bathroom, and I would hear his tinkling —
this exacerbating my own urgency. Next the sound of the faucet as
he rinsed the sleep from his face. Then Mother went to the bathroom.

After all of this, which seemed hours long, they tiptoed into
our rooms, opening fully the already ajar doors and softly calling,
"Merrrry Christmas."

We children rushed into slippers and robes, but rush as we did,
we knew not to go into the living room until invited. At first the
parents asked if we needed to go to the bathroom. In spite of prior
urgencies, we didn't. Then my mother would make a short speech
about the true meaning of Christmas. It is the Lord's day, she said.
"We are celebrating the salvation of the world brought to us by a
child." The speech was not awfully long, twenty-five words or
less, but it seemed an interminable cruelty at that moment. Then
Daddy swung Josie into his arms and rubbed his whiskers against
her face. "Come along, my pretty baby," he said, and the fun
began.

❧

About ten o'clock, we received visitors. My favorite visitor was
Mr. Rodriguez, the hot tamale man. Mother loved his hot tamales,
which during the summer he brought around every afternoon in a
pedal cart. He began his visit by announcing he was just poking his
head in the door to say hello. He was a tall yellow man with
straight hair, and people said he had some white blood in him.
Mother said that he was Mexican, and that if he wanted to, he
could pass for white. But he used to be married to a colored
woman and so he went for Negro instead. Why anybody would
want to go for Negro in Birmingham, Mother said, was a mystery.
I guess love is the mystery, Father mused. Mother offered Mr.
Rodriguez a glass of eggnog — no liquor in it at that time of
morning — although Father offered liquor. Mr. Rodriguez asked
Josie if he could have a look at her dolls, and when she brought

them to him he made do over them, patted her on the head, and then made do over her. Mr. Rodriguez, eggnog on his mustache, cocked his head and looked at the ceiling. What exactly he was looking at was not clear. Josie pulled away from him and retreated to where Mother sat, and Father, sitting across from Mr. Rodriguez, talked about the weather.

"You know, Mr. Burke," Mr. Rodriguez said, ignoring the forecast of snow in January, "I lost my family a few years back. June 7, 1948."

"Yes, Mr. Rodriguez, you have told me many times, and I am so sorry for your loss. Time heals all wounds."

Mr. Rodriguez smiled faintly. He still focused on the ceiling. "All wounds? I've yet to see a wound that time has healed. Some things you never get over."

Mother went to the kitchen, Josie tagging behind her, and returned with a plate of cookies that she placed on the coffee table in front of Mr. Rodriguez. She stood a moment and wiped her hands on her apron, looking first at Mr. Rodriguez and then at my father. Something about her air caused me to look up from the star chart I was studying. She seemed deep in thought, as if her voice wasn't her own but one channeling through her. She announced to us all, not just Mr. Rodriguez, "Loss is a part of this world." After a moment, the hot tamale man agreed.

About noon my father packed the car for the ride to Grandma Pic's. He filled the trunk with covered dishes of food, among them Mother's Christmas specialty, hot cross buns, and boxes wrapped in bright paper and pretty bows. Each child was allowed to bring just one toy to show. My telescope was too large, and because it really wasn't a toy, after all, I took my book, *The Golden Encyclopedia of Science*. I knew I wouldn't have time to read it once I got to Grandma Pic's house, but the oversized book full of colorful pictures was still good for show.

Just before two we arrived at Grandma Pic's house near Cusada, a crossroads in the floodplain of the Alabama River outside of Montgomery. During these family gatherings, the women prepared the supper, the men talked with glasses of bourbon resting on their knees, and the children were banned from the house. We romped in Grandma Pic's sprawling, weedy front yard, swung from the low limbs of the many crepe myrtles, mimosas, and dogwoods, and played hide-and-seek among the rows of boxwoods, tea olives, and azaleas. Across the graveled road in front of the house was a woods we were forbidden to enter. It belonged to a white farmer whom Grandma Pic had made into a bogeyman. If we ventured into the road, he would know it, even if she didn't. If we went into those woods, he would "get" us. "What would he do to us?" we implored. "Don't worry about what he will do to you," she returned as a haughty answer. "It won't be as bad as what I will do to you."

We played outdoors until we got cold, then we were shooed into the upstairs of the old wooden house, to a bedroom where Mother and her sister, Aunt Benni, used to sleep. I had five cousins, all younger than myself, although only Vachel — we called him Vak — was an actual first cousin, Aunt Benni's son. The others were Uncle Reed's grandchildren — Uncle Reed and Grandma Pic were living without benefit of marriage.

Inside was noisy, cramped, and warm. The men — Uncle Reed and his two sons-in-law, Uncle William, who was Aunt Benni's husband, and my father — talked loudly about sports, travel, farming — all of which was really the same subject: politics. Whether they were talking about Jackie Robinson and baseball or the Alabama-Georgia football rig, they were talking politics. Uncle William and Aunt Benni's drive from Philadelphia was political. "Once you cross ole Mason and Dixon, you can't even find a place to pee, much less sleep," Uncle William proclaimed, taking some satisfaction that he would soon cross back the other way. They were careful to plan the car trip so that they traveled the southern states during the daylight. The men's plain-tive voices could be heard through the plank floors, so that even though we children were scooting about on our knees as we played with Tonka trucks and speed racers, we were aware, at least in tone, of the political debate of the day.

We children had less privilege to hear the women's talk. Often they hushed when we entered the kitchen or dining room. I sus-pect they talked less about the flavor of paprika than the spicy goings-on between neighbors and others in the family. Sometimes the affair would be so unsavory as to leave Grandma Pic stunned. She sat heavily and shook her head. Nonetheless, this talk was pol-itics, too.

Just about the time we children remembered we were hungry, we took notice of the inviting smells coming from the kitchen. Sweet potatoes were a specialty of Grandma Pic's. She raised them, she covered them with lime and stored them on elevated shelves in the corn shed. She separated the cured ones from the green ones, and she cooked them in just about any way it was possible to cook one. No *Southern Living* recipe could match her potato casserole. The potatoes were sliced and layered in the dish, and between the layers was a creamy, buttery, nut-flavored pudding of sweet potatoes, nutmeg, and cinnamon. The very top layer was a crust of crunchy pecans — these gathered aggressively from Grandma Pic's one tree. Not a single nut was ever lost to a squirrel.

Finishing a first helping of Christmas supper was no easy task: turkey; cornbread dressing with giblet gravy, another of Grandma Pic's specialties; Uncle Reed's cured ham, soaked and boiled and baked. Vegetables galore: beets, green beans freshly canned from the summer crop, rutabagas, and turnips — "You don't need both!" Mother protested, but Grandma Pic waved away any sug-gestion of frugality — collards and turnip greens, candied carrots, stewed canned tomatoes, and bread made by one of Uncle Reed's daughters (of whom I had heard Grandma Pic say, "She can't cook, but she tries hard"); my mother's cross buns, Aunt Benni's cornbread, pickled peaches, homemade applesauce, canned cranberry gelatin — alas, the only concession to store-bought. But this was only the first course. A dessert course offering bread pudding and lemon sauce, fruitcake, butter-rich pound cake, canned peaches in heavy syrup, and of course sweet potato pie would come last.

The dishes rarely fit on the table at one time, and Grandma Pic was up and down, running between the kitchen and the dining room, serving food for the other adults, who sat thigh to thigh at the table. Children, of course, sat at the children's table — the kitchen table — but we were only a few feet from the adults, clearly visible to our watchful parents, and able to hear every word they said.

"Now I hear y'all gone raise some kind of trouble up in Birmingham," Uncle Reed said between bites.

"What's that?" my father said, and then to my mother, "Honey, pass the pickled peaches, please," and to my grandmother, "Piccadilly, my dear, you have gone and outdone yourself. Truly, you have."

"You would think King Wenceslas or somebody was coming to eat," Aunt Benni said with a laugh, and then without missing a beat she admonished my cousin at the children's table, "Vachel, you had betta not waste that food — all those poor, starving children over in India."

"Ain't nobody starving 'round here," Grandma Pic offered in defense. She turned to Vachel. "Vachel, baby, what you need? You need something?"

"He don' need nothing, Mama. Need a whipping, that's just all."

"Yeah, I hear tell the Reverend Martin Luther King's coming up to Birmingham," Uncle Reed continued as if there had been no interruption. "I hear he's fixin' to set them white people straight." Uncle pointed his fork at my father.

"I hadn't heard." Daddy made a pensive pause. "I suppose there will be a mess."

"What's that?" Mother asked.

"Mess?" Uncle Reed talked with his mouth full. "He made a mess in Albany, and folks ain't one bit better off than before he came. Folks still in jail."

"Well, without a struggle . . ." one of Uncle Reed's sons-in-law started.

"Struggle my behind!" Uncle Reed pointed his fork again. "You struggling and them crackers will be kicking your back part."

"What's going on?" Mother asked again.

"King's coming to Birmingham," Daddy answered.

"King who?" Aunt Benni asked.

"King of England," Daddy answered. I saw his lips quiver, trying to hold back his smile, and then he took a big bite of food and chewed hard.

"Ain't fixin' to do nothing but stir up a hornets' nest. Those crazy crackers will be throwing dynamite again. Ain't no Birmingham . . ." Uncle Reed shook his fork. "It's Bombingham. Them crazy crackers made it Bombingham."

"Put your fork down!" Grandma Pic ordered. "This is Christmas. Can't we have one day without complaining about white folks?"

Grandma Pic's tone quieted the conversation for a moment. Then Aunt Benni began to chuckle. She wagged her finger at Father, who sat across from her. "King of England? King of England? There is no king of England."

"There sure 'nough is," Grandma Pic said as she rose, picked up an empty bowl, and came into the kitchen.

"England has a *queen*," Aunt Benni corrected.

"I don't care," Grandma Pic said. Then she patted me on the shoulder. "I'm the queen around here. Ain't I, Walter, baby?"

"Yes ma'am."

She held the empty bowl over her head with one hand and

mocked a regal pose. "See my crown. I'm the queen in this house, and them in there are my subjects." We children giggled — the grownups did too, for in that sliver of time we were a royal family, as rich and as far away from trouble as we wanted to be.

Remembering that moment, seeing in my mind the glow of satisfaction on the faces of my relatives and the pride and happiness with which Grandma Pic paraded around the kitchen, I have come to understand that as happy as it was, and as happy as I am to remember it, it was nonetheless a footing on which grief would be built. It is also clearer to me what I feel on this day of national mourning. It is not grief but fear — the fear of the loss of happy times, which, as we all know, is inevitable. Praise God!

 Ba-chan's Superstition

1948

My older sister, Kimi, was graduating from high school. For a week she had moped around the apartment, speaking to no one, locking herself in the bedroom she shared with me and our grandmother. You'd think she would have been ecstatic not having to go to school anymore.

"Ba-chan, what's the matter with Kimi?"

Grandmother hesitated before answering. "She mad because no have silk stocking for graduate."

"Why? Won't Mama and Papa let her wear them?" I suspected our old-fashioned parents thought silk stockings were too sexy.

"Cost too much. Too much money." Ba-chan's thin lips drooped at the corners and her faded eyes seemed to fill with tears.

I knew we were poor, but surely not so poverty-stricken we couldn't afford some silk hose for something so auspicious as graduation. Our parents worked at the fish cannery every day, leaving Grandma to care for Kimi, myself, and my younger brother, Ken. After the war the government had placed us and other Japanese American families in Cabrillo Homes, a low-rent housing project built during the war for defense workers. The apartments were small and spartan, with the front door leading immediately into a kitchen equipped with stove, icebox, and small table. But the apartment seemed luxurious compared to the internment camp barracks we left in Arizona.

There was enough to eat. But then, Ba-chan was exceptionally thrifty. Always preparing for the worst, she saved everything — rags, strings wound into balls, jars, paper bags, magazines. The closets were stuffed with her treasures, overflowing into cardboard boxes hidden under beds and stacked against the living room walls, so that the apartment looked more like a warehouse than a home.

"Hasn't Kimi started working at the gift shop downtown on weekends? She should be making some money to buy hose."

Ba-chan nodded. "But we need money."

I hadn't realized Kimi's measly wages added to the family fund. I felt a twinge of guilt and wished I could help her somehow. I understood how important it was to look like the other kids. It would be humiliating to graduate with naked legs . . . or, worse, to wear leg makeup like Mrs. Novak, who lived in the next apartment. Mrs. Novak's legs were thick round pillars, streaked rosy beige and crisscrossed with splinters of dark hair. When she lumbered past the kitchen window each morning, high-heeled wedgies scuffing the sidewalk, Kimi and I stared in amazement at the pink elephant legs, unevenly smudged with chalky lotion.

One day there was a knock on the door, soft and hesitant. I opened the door and was surprised to see a beautiful young woman, who smiled warmly at me.

"I'm Chiye Oda," she said in a deep, melodious voice. "I work with Kimi at the gift shop, and I've brought a graduation present for her." She handed me a colorfully wrapped package.

"How nice," I cooed. "Won't you come in?" Since she was Japanese, I wasn't ashamed to invite her into our pungent-smelling apartment; Ba-chan's tsukemono (fermenting vegetables in wooden crocks) and drying fish sequestered in one of the bedrooms wouldn't be shocking or offensive.

"Oh, no, thank you," she said politely, looking past me to Ba-chan standing by the kitchen table. She backed away. "Just tell Kimi congratulations and I'll see her at work."

I saw she limped, one leg noticeably shorter and stiff from the hip down. But her walk was graceful, almost sinuous, as I watched her glide down the sidewalk and disappear around the corner. Dazzled by her beauty, I became envious of Kimi's friendship.

"Let me see present," said Ba-chan in an unusual harsh voice.

"Can't I give it to Kimi?"

"Give me first!" She grabbed the package and shuffled to the tokonoma (our family shrine set on a shelf in the living room). After laying it before Kamisama, the small bronze Buddha sitting in repose, she lit some incense and began chanting with hands clasped in front of her chest. She waved the package over the rising incense fumes and then blew on it three times. Puff. Puff. Puff.

"Okay, now. All clean. Can give to Kimi."

Chiye's gift was a pair of silk hose. Kimi was in heaven, and her cheery mood prompted me to ask questions I dared not ask Ba-chan.

"You know, Ba-chan did a whole cleansing thing at the tokonoma. Why would she pray over Chiye's present?"

Kimi's brown eyes turned black and liquid, mysterious pools of dark light. She locked the bedroom door. "If you ever get to know Chiye, don't you dare utter a word to her. Promise?"

"I promise."

Kimi whispered, "Ba-chan is afraid of Chiye and her family."

"Why?" I hissed back. "Are they bad luck?"

"Something like that. Ba-chan says Chiye is crippled because she had tuberculosis."

"What's that?" I remembered Mama and Papa talking about it in hushed tones. They were secretive, fearful, as if the word itself had power and by just speaking it they were conjuring an evil force.

Kimi's black eyes penetrated mine. "It's a disease," she whispered fiercely. "But Japanese think it's a curse. Ba-chan says it's inherited because of some sin in the family's past. Bad karma. Makes you crippled and crazy and kills you. And *everyone* dies who gets it!"

Dismayed, I scarcely could ask, "Do you believe that, Kimi?" I remembered how beautiful and healthy Chiye looked.

"Of course not. TB is a very catchy disease, and families got it because they lived close together in crowded conditions in Japan."

I was relieved and then angry. "Then how cruel to treat them like outcasts!" I thought of Chiye's kindness to Kimi.

"I know. But it's hard to change centuries of superstition. Now don't you dare mention what I've said to Chiye."

I vowed secrecy and was now eager to know Chiye even more and determined to atone in some way for Ba-chan's cruel narrow-mindedness.

After graduation, Kimi moved out of the apartment to work as a mother's helper in a rich doctor's home across town. I wanted to take over her job at the gift shop, but fourteen was too young. I wished I had lied about my age when I applied after Kimi left.

But I discovered another way to get to know Chiye. I found out where she lived from Mrs. Sato, our gossipy neighbor, who knew everyone and everything Japanese in Cabrillo Homes.

I slipped out of the apartment one night, a more than usually foggy night, the air a thick gray blanket muffling the plaintive moan of a distant foghorn. Protected by the damp mist, I walked the many blocks to Chiye's tenement apartment.

The dark stairway smelled of mold and faintly of urine. At the landing I heard music and a sultry voice singing an unfamiliar tune. I tapped on the door, which held a wooden sign: ODA.

Chiye opened the door. "Well, hi, Reiko. Come in." She seemed genuinely pleased to see me and not at all surprised.

The living room was lit by a blue light. After becoming accustomed to the eerie blueness, I realized several people were sitting on the bare wooden floor. Two men held guitars.

"I'm sorry. I didn't know you were having a party."

Chiye had picked up a ukelele and strummed it with long red

fingernails. "Don't worry. We're just practicing, making music. You can be our audience." She laughed softly and began to sing. I sat on the floor and watched in wonder while they played and sang well into the night.

From then on I was at Chiye's every chance I had. I sneaked over in the evenings, lying to Ba-chan that I was going to Lupe's, my Mexican friend's. Chiye had a younger sister and brother, but there was no sign of parents.

I learned to play the uke. Many evenings we sat for hours strumming and singing popular tunes of the forties — "Harbor Lights," "My Destiny," "The Old Lamplighter." She introduced the magazines *Modern Romance* and *True Love* and told me about the birds and bees, filling in details not discussed by kids my own age. I learned to shave my legs, and she permed my hair and painted my finger- and toenails with bright red polish, which I carefully removed before I went home. She was my idol, a goddess of the sensual arts, and best of all, a true and worldly friend.

For months the apprenticeship continued. I was always careful to wipe off the lipstick and rouge before I left her apartment. But one day, after she had plucked my eyebrows and splashed a strong-smelling cologne called Tabu on my hair, Ba-chan wrinkled her nose and peered with squinting eyes.

"Why you stink funny?"

I thought fast. "Oh, Lupe's mother put perfume on me." I ducked past Ba-chan into the bathroom, hoping she wouldn't notice my newly arched eyebrows. But she was uncanny — sometimes psychic.

"You no see Chiye? Kimi's friend?" she yelled at the bathroom door.

"Who? . . . Oh, you mean the girl who gave Kimi the silk stockings?" My heart thumped.

Ba-chan yelled louder. "They bad luck. Bad karma. No mama, no papa. Everybody die. Bad thing . . . TB."

Fury welled in my chest. Why was Ba-chan so cruel? Chiye

was kinder than anyone I ever had known. Even if her parents had died from the disease, it didn't make them criminals! I cried quietly, swallowing my rage. But a small part of me was afraid — afraid for Chiye. I prayed Ba-chan was wrong, just a superstitious old lady who didn't want me to have any fun.

A few weeks later I came down with strep throat and was in bed for two weeks, too sick to even think of my glamorous mentor. When I recovered I hurried to her house and climbed the musty stairs, a cold feeling sweeping over me as I saw the sign ODA was gone. I knocked. No answer. I knocked louder, waiting for the uneven tapping of Chiye's gait. Silence. I ran to Mrs. Sato's and she reported, rather smugly, that the Odas had moved away. "Just like that," she clucked. "Overnight they were gone. Nobody knows where."

I was devastated. I waited patiently for some word from her, certain she would write. But the days turned into weeks and then months. I finally gave up hope.

❧

It was nearing Christmas. I had joined a church club that planned to sing carols for local orphanages and hospitals. We practiced after school, our lilting voices floating over the drab stucco buildings of the project. I loved that time of year, and imagined the dense fog was pure snow, crystal flakes that transformed the cement into a wintery landscape.

On performance day, the bus creaked to the county hospital outside of town, whose low-slung buildings looked like the internment camp barracks in Arizona.

Inside, as we passed the open entrance of a wing designated QUARANTINE, I heard a voice call out. I thought I heard my name. Peering down the patient-filled wing, I saw a white-gowned figure sitting in bed and waving. It was Chiye. Her face was full and she looked heavier, but her smile was the same. I began to run down the hall, but a nurse grabbed my arm.

"You mustn't enter this wing," she said, guiding me back to the group. "It's for tuberculosis patients."

The awful words sank in. In a trance I waved back to Chiye, who continued fluttering her slim hand. She then blew a kiss as we moved on.

For months after the incident, I was distraught. I wanted to forget the hospital, what it meant, hoping somehow it was all a dream, a vision conjured up by Ba-chan. The secret weighed heavily, and in my grief I blamed Ba-chan and her beliefs for Chiye's death. Finally, after a year, I accepted that Chiye was dead and erased any memory of her.

Twenty years later I was traveling on Highway 101 in California and stopped at a small café to break up the long trip from San Francisco to Los Angeles. It was in a small town outside of Santa Maria, almost halfway between the two cities.

I sat alone in a booth, savoring a hot bowl of split pea soup, when a voice called out from across the room.

"Reiko? Aren't you Reiko?"

A middle-aged woman sitting in another booth — also alone — smiled at me. Brownish hair coiled loosely in a French roll, with wisps of gray, framed an oval Asian face. The low, throaty voice reverberated in my memory somewhere.

"Can I join you?"

I was hesitant, not knowing whether to be annoyed or receptive to this strangely familiar woman. "Of course," I said, wondering how she knew my name.

She slid from the booth and walked toward me, her slender body rising and falling in a rolling gait. I froze. Was I seeing a ghost?

"Chiye?" I managed to whisper. "Could you really be Chiye?"

"That's right. I'm glad you remember me." The small black eyes twinkled. "For a moment I thought you didn't. It's been a long time. But you haven't changed one bit, Reiko."

Overcome, I began to cry. Was I experiencing a miracle?

"Goodness, you'd think I'd come back from the grave."

I couldn't speak.

"I wrote several cards from the hospital. Remember? That's where I last saw you. When you didn't answer, I figured your family didn't want you to keep in touch." She paused. "You know how Japanese are about TB." Her voice was soft with forgiveness.

Ba-chan! She must have intercepted the letters!

"We moved up here to Santa Maria after I became well," she continued, seeming oblivious to my unresponsiveness.

I thought of work-worn Ba-chan, forever the survivor, struggling to keep the family together, befuddled by a culture that placed the same value on silk stockings as it did on food. For years I had been so angry with Ba-chan and her stubborn way of seeing things. But Chiye had not died after all! Here she was, still as beautiful, full of warmth and acceptance.

I found my voice. "Yes, Grandma was so eccentric. But I'm sure she thought nothing of you having TB. She was getting a little senile then, and I'm sure she put your letters in the tsukemono crock or icebox. Once I found cans of Campbell's soup in my underwear drawer!"

We both laughed aloud.

I stayed a couple of hours longer at the café, and we chatted about the past twenty years of our lives as if our chance reunion had been planned to fill in that empty space.

CHANG-RAE LEE

 # Mute in an English-Only World

When I read of the troubles in Palisades Park, New Jersey, over the proliferation of Korean-language signs along its main commercial strip, I unexpectedly sympathized with the frustrations, resentments, and fears of the longtime residents. They clearly felt alienated and even unwelcome in a vital part of their community. The town, like seven others in New Jersey, has passed laws requiring that half of any commercial sign in a foreign language be in English.

Now I certainly would never tolerate any exclusionary ideas about who could rightfully settle and belong in the town. But having been raised in a Korean immigrant family, I saw every day the exacting price and power of language, especially with my mother, who was an outsider in an English-only world. In the first years we lived in America, my mother could speak only the most basic English, and she often encountered great difficulty whenever she went out.

We lived in New Rochelle, New York, in the early seventies, and most of the local businesses were run by the descendants of immigrants who, generations ago, had come to the suburbs from New York City. Proudly dotting Main Street and North Avenue were Italian pastry and cheese shops, Jewish tailors and cleaners, and Polish and German butchers and bakers. If my mother's marketing couldn't wait until the weekend, when my father had free time, she would often hold off until I came home from school to buy the groceries.

Though I was only six or seven years old, she insisted that I go out shopping with her and my younger sister. I mostly loathed the task, partly because it meant I couldn't spend the afternoon off playing catch with my friends but also because I knew our errands would inevitably lead to an awkward scene, and that I would have to speak up to help my mother.

I was just learning the language myself, but I was a quick study, as children are with new tongues. I had spent kindergarten in almost complete silence, hearing only the high nasality of my teacher and comprehending little but the cranky wails and cries of my classmates. But soon, seemingly mere months later, I had already become a terrible ham and mimic, and I would crack up my father with impressions of teachers, his friends, and even himself. My mother scolded me for aping his speech, and the one time I attempted to make light of hers I rated a roundhouse smack on my bottom.

For her, the English language was not very funny. It usually meant trouble and a good dose of shame, and sometimes real hurt. Although she had a good reading knowledge of the language from university classes in South Korea, she had never practiced actual conversation. So in America she used English flash cards and phrase books and watched television with us kids. And she faithfully carried a pocket workbook illustrated with stick-figure people and compound sentences to be filled in.

But none of it seemed to do her much good. Staying mostly at home to care for us, she didn't have many chances to try out sundry words and phrases. When she did, say, at the window of the post office, her readied speech would stall, freeze, sometimes altogether collapse.

One day was unusually harrowing. We ventured downtown in the new Ford Country Squire my father had bought her, an enormous station wagon that seemed as long — and deft — as an ocean liner. We were shopping for a special meal for guests visiting that weekend, and my mother had heard that a particular butcher carried fresh oxtails, which she needed for a traditional soup.

We'd never been inside the shop, but my mother would pause before its window, which was always lined with whole hams, crown roasts, and ropes of plump handmade sausages. She greatly esteemed the bounty with her eyes, and my sister and I did also, but despite our desirous cries she'd turn us away and instead buy the packaged links at the Finast supermarket, where she felt comfortable looking them over and could easily spot the price. And, of course, not have to talk.

But that day she was resolved. The butcher store was crowded, and as we stepped inside the door jingled a welcome. No one seemed to notice. We waited for some time, and people who entered after us were now being served. Finally an old woman nudged my mother and waved a little ticket, which we hadn't taken. We patiently waited again, until one of the beefy men behind the glass display hollered our number.

My mother pulled us forward and began searching the cases, but the oxtails were nowhere to be found. The man, his big arms crossed, sharply said, "Come on, lady, whaddya want?" This unnerved her, and she somehow blurted the Korean word for oxtail, *soggori.*

The butcher looked as if my mother had put something sour in his mouth, and he glanced back at the lighted board and called the next number.

Before I knew it, she had rushed us outside and back in the wagon, which she had double-parked because of the crowd. She was furious, almost vibrating with fear and grief, and I could see she was about to cry.

She wanted to go back inside, but now the driver of the car we were blocking wanted to pull out. She was shooing us away. My mother, who had just earned her driver's license, started furiously working the pedals. But in her haste she must have flooded the engine, for it wouldn't turn over. The driver started honking and then another car began honking as well, and soon it seemed the entire street was shrieking at us.

In the following years, my mother grew steadily more comfortable with English. In Korean she could be fiery, stern, deeply funny, and ironic, in English just slightly less so. If she was never quite fluent, she gained enough confidence to make herself clearly known to anyone, and particularly to me.

Five years ago she died of cancer, and some months after we buried her I found myself in the driveway of my father's house, washing her sedan. I liked taking care of her things; it made me feel close to her. While I was cleaning out the glove compartment, I found her pocket English workbook, the one with the silly illustrations. I hadn't seen it in nearly twenty years. The yellowed pages were brittle and dog-eared. She had fashioned a plain paper wrapping for it, and I wondered whether she meant to protect the book or hide it.

I don't doubt that she would have appreciated doing the family shopping on the new Broad Avenue of Palisades Park. But I like to think, too, that she would have understood those who now complain about the Korean-only signs.

I wonder what these same people would have done if they had seen my mother studying her English workbook — or lost in a store. Would they have nodded gently at her? Would they have lent a kind word?

 Memphis Years

I remember practically none of this. My mother told me the stories late in her life. Some of it I discovered even later, in a notebook she kept when, clearly, she knew she was dying. There she described how I came by my name, after she saw the photograph of a debutante named Beverly on the society page of the Sunday *Commercial-Appeal*. It was "different," she said. She liked that.

I was born in the Baptist Hospital in Memphis, where we lived on Walker Street in a duplex my mother and father bought, one of only two houses they would ever own and the only one they would voluntarily sell. My father, she said, was gone all the time in those days, attending pharmacy school, working at a drugstore during the week and on weekends, moonlighting on the Peabody Hotel roof as a combination bouncer and featured four-string banjo player, sitting in with whatever famous band was in town. (Once, when he was in his seventies and an old jump tune came on the car radio, he asked me to turn it up; it was a song he used to dance to as part of the act. When the beat hit, he'd set his banjo aside, jump to his feet, and do a solo bump-and-grind boogie that cleared the floor.) When he found out a baby was on the way, he asked to install a nickel pinball machine in the drugstore, the profits of which would go to pay for my birth. And so, or this is how the story goes, I entered life named for a Memphis debutante, my birth paid for in nickels my father dumped into a paper sack and emptied on somebody's desk.

We lived in Memphis until I was three. Photographs of me there show an impy little girl in white boots, all forehead, wild-eyed and lively. My mother said that in those years I was a pistol, mischievous, sparky, always running away, down city sidewalks into alleys and around unknown corners, while she took her afternoon nap. When she told me this I was amazed. As far back as I could clearly remember I'd been such a good girl: teacher's dream, repressed, virginal, teetotaler, scared. What happened?

My mother was blue-eyed, pale, terrified of water, loved cigarettes, hated school. In the days of pageboys, her thick blond hair folded into a seamless roll. She and I were very different in many ways. Like my father, I was dark-eyed, wispy-haired; summers my skin turned pecan brown, and once I learned to swim I never wanted to do anything else. School was my refuge and I loved it. I always thought sleeping was for nighttime, couldn't nap as a child and still don't. But on the sunniest day my mother could lay her head on a pillow and in a couple of breaths sink down and be gone, happy as if off to meet a lover. And that was when, she said, I'd slip from her grasp and take off. She'd wake up to find the bed empty, the house all quiet. She'd run outside, yelling my name. And eventually somebody, she said, showed up with me in tow, maybe wearing those white boots, I don't know. I wasn't scared or sorry, she reported, just smelly. Apparently every time I ran away I filled my underpants. And that was how I was in the Memphis years, a runaway dirty girl, on the prowl for secret adventures.

She was pregnant at that time, and when my brother was born, she said, I changed. At three, I became a regular little nursemaid, watching over him. That was how she said it for a long time, either leaving out or denying the crucial part, because as I see it, he wasn't the one I was trying to take care of.

In that same year — the summer of 1941 — my mother contracted polio. No one knew what was wrong with her; no one seriously tried to find out, mainly because she was already in the Baptist Hospital at the time, giving birth to my brother. And so doctors diagnosed milk leg or postpartum blues, reckoning that the paralysis and excruciating pain she was in had to do with child-birth, a woman's thing; how could it not? When she told me all of this, I asked her if these diagnoses angered her. She said all she could think about was the pain.

By then my father had finished school and gotten a straight job working as a pharmacist in Clarksdale, Mississippi, in the Delta, about an hour and a half from Memphis. When my mother was released from the hospital, the four of us went there to live, and my father hired a woman to help take care of us. My mother said that the only thing that relieved her pain was when the woman dropped a towel in boiling water, then wrapped it around her right leg. My father brought home a heat lamp, which she said also helped. And finally he took her back to Memphis, where the doctor took one look at her and said, "My God. You've already been through it," and my father wept at his own ignorance and blind faith in doctors.

They laced her foot in a clunky brown boot and buckled her leg in a metal brace they said she'd wear from then on, but she didn't. She was vain and a looker, not about to crip around in a thick ugly boot the rest of her life. In pictures from that time, her right leg is hidden, tucked behind the left, and you can't see the brace. In time she threw it away and found snappy shoes she could manage to walk in, usually Jack Rogers wedgies, which to me had a kind of outlandish Florida look.

We moved around a lot, from Clarksdale back to Memphis and then to Arkansas for a while. Eventually we ended up back in the Mississippi Delta, in one rented house after another in Greenville, where I pursued and attained good grades and a fifties version of don't-touch girl perfection.

Childhood, of course, never ends. After I stopped running away, I took to eating dirt. It's said I especially liked the soft black stuff found in the huge flowerpots that flanked my grandmother's front steps. I vaguely recall the dark taste and the feel of grit between my teeth, my forbidden pleasure. Daddy said whenever I went off behind the bushes, he knew. "Eating dirt, Bev?" he'd ask, and I'd shake my head and spit out the dirt, but when I turned around my mouth was ringed in black. I didn't date or dance much in my high school or college years, but later on, when I finally rediscovered my Memphis self and put on my dancing shoes, I followed in the footsteps of my father when he did that lowdown boogie on the roof of the Peabody Hotel. It's like running away in jazzy white boots, but this time with somebody instead of in secret, and to music. In a novel I wrote, when a character named Sue is asked how she deals with heartache, she says, "Turn up the music and dance."

MICHAEL PATRICK MacDONALD
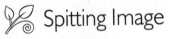 Spitting Image

I was looking at my father for the first time ever. Ma says we'd met when I was a baby, but I don't remember. I was nineteen now, and until this night I could only imagine what he might look like, the way some people imagine ancestors from family stories. I knew I was looking at my father for the last time, too, and no matter how hard I looked, I couldn't see the resemblance to myself. And I had gone there looking for something familiar. He was, after all, my father; and I was his only kid.

I don't know what I expected to find. But as far back as I could remember, I'd heard aunts with folded arms whisper stories about George Fox being Ma's only decent boyfriend, then nod their heads among general agreement that I was the spitting image of the man that Ma would have done good to marry. They'd said he was tall, smart, and with a "big job" at the navy yard. Why Ma would marry a no-good blackguard the like of Dave MacDonald, the wife-beating father of my eight older brothers and sisters, and not hold on to George Fox, Grandpa said he'd never know. This was said at tea, only among aunts and uncles who knew I wasn't really a MacDonald, since Grandpa and Nana were from the old country, where there was no such thing as running off with all kinds of men and having illegitimate babies. My grandparents were good to me; still, "Your mother has no shame, no shame at all" was the refrain I listened to throughout childhood as I sipped sweet milky tea from their saucers and wondered how great my father must be.

My brothers and sisters knew George, since he'd stayed at the apartment in Columbia Point Project for a few months after I was born, and they too seemed to like him all right, better than any of Ma's other boyfriends. They all reminisced with Ma about the one time that Mac, their father, walked into the apartment for a rare visit, only to come face to face with George at the threshold. Davey, the oldest, who hated Mac, made it sound to me like a Jackie Gleason episode where the two were stuck in the doorway, trying to pass in opposite directions. They all agreed that George was a head over Mac as they crossed paths, glaring and never saying a word. Mary said George Fox took all the kids to Santa's Village a couple years in a row; and to hear Mary, an adult mother of three, talk with big eyes about the elves and real reindeer and the rides through the North Pole, you'd swear George Fox was just about the greatest man that ever set foot in the project. My sister Mary liked him enough even to come along with me now, to see him one more time. To pay her respects.

"Looks like he was a smoker," Mary whispered as we knelt at his side. Mary hadn't seen George in maybe eighteen years. She scrunched her forehead, nodding toward his stiff hands folded into each other and wrapped in rosaries. Mary and I had buried three brothers through my teen years, and had seen many neighbors waked, every one of them looking like he had died saying a rosary, so I couldn't figure what she was carrying on about. I looked at George's hands and then back at Mary. "Tobacco stains," she muttered out the side of her mouth, pointing now, quickly, toward his fingernails. She said it wasn't at all like him to be a smoker. She said he had seemed more sensible than that. She then stood up and leaned slightly into the casket, looking for God knows what. Mary was a nurse in the OR at Boston City Hospital, so she was a great one for making casual observations on a corpse; "the detective" is what the other nurses called her at work. I'd often found myself tuning out her horrific work tales of car wrecks and body parts, made more horrific by her matter-of-fact tone. My stomach had been in knots the whole drive to the wake; and now, looking at my father's tobacco stains, I was feeling sicker. Still, I *was* listening to Mary as we both blessed ourselves to pray. Instead of praying, I pictured the dead man before me smoking away and wondered whether I would make it to the toilet.

I wouldn't know, I thought, shrugging off any sign of interest. I had decided in that moment that I had no connection at all to George Fox, that it was too late. The churning in my stomach went away completely. Then Mary went silent to finish up the praying, so that George Fox's friends, or relatives, or whoever they were in the line behind us, could have their turn. I turned my head to look behind me at a room full of strangers huddled in circles, shaking their heads and telling stories that all ended with exclamations of "I just saw him last Friday!" or "I just saw him three days ago!" Whenever it was that they'd last seen him, they were sure to let everyone know, opening their arms as if to include people beyond their own circle of listeners, who couldn't believe someone they'd *just* seen was now dead. Some of the men — the ones with greaser hairdos from their heydays, favorite dungarees, and baseball jackets with "Blarney Stone" or "Mickey's Pub" stretched on broad backs — had even seen him just minutes before his death. "There he was at the bar, big as life, healthy as a horse, and generous as the day is long, ordering a round for everyone," one of the ladies with Elvis Presley hair recounted of George's last minutes. She said, had she known when he got up for the toilet that he'd not be coming back . . . She looked at the floor and shook her head in disbelief before straightening up to deliver the punch line: "I'd've made the bastard pay for the round *before* he went to the john!" A whole corner of the room, those who seemed to know George Fox better than anyone, erupted into fits of laughter, holding their sides for fear of splitting. For some, laughter released tears that I knew mightn't have come out any other way. It was all looking very familiar to me. We were in Dorchester, and even though it was the next neighborhood over from our own Southie, I'd never realized until now just how close to home my father's wake was. Half the room emptied for a smoke on the front steps, and the laughter and uncontrollable coughing became distant, only to come pouring in every time someone else opened the front door to go for a smoke. I turned back to George's face in front of me, and though I still probably looked like I couldn't have cared less, I was now waiting for Mary to finish praying and tell me more about the stranger in a casket.

We blessed ourselves again, even though I'd forgotten to say a single Our Father.

Mary said something about George's being "normal," and that's when I thought my whole stomach would pass through my throat. In recent years I'd decided that "normal" certainly meant something somewhere out there, beyond the Old Colony Project, where we lived. I looked at the corpse in front of me and felt my neck beginning to sweat, although I felt cold. From all the talk I'd heard over the years about George Fox — always referred to by his full name — and his "big job" inspecting ships at the navy yard, he seemed like some strange sensible man who wouldn't have nicotine stains on his fingers and wouldn't be the type to ignore his kid who lived in a housing project or to die puking in the toilet at the Emerald Isle, only a couple miles, in a straight line down Dorchester Avenue, from Old Colony Project. My mother had mentioned seeing him on occasion, when she played accordion at the Emerald Isle, and that he'd asked, "How's Michael?" as they passed each other in the crowd. She told me that she'd given him our number a couple of times. And in more recent years, every time any of my brothers died and it was splashed all over the papers about falls from rooftops, bank robberies, or a mysterious prison death, I went to their wakes keeping a nervous eye out for George Fox, who surely had read about my family dying in Old Colony. None of them were his kids, but still, they were my brothers. I didn't know how I'd react if he did come to my brothers' wakes. When my oldest brother, Davey, committed suicide, I was thirteen and still imagined knowing George. When my sister

Kathy was pushed off the project roof in a struggle over pills, I was fourteen and losing interest in him. By the time Frankie's and Kevin's deaths — eight months apart — were hitting the *Boston Herald* in splashy crime stories, I was sixteen, and I remember thinking on the way to one of their wakes that it was too late to get to know a "father" and that if the coward ever showed up I'd probably stab him as soon as look at him.

I suddenly felt like my blood was heating up through my entire body, spreading to head, hands, and feet. The rush actually felt good. For a moment I thought I might be truly evil, thinking these things just seconds after making the sign of the cross at a casket, but at least my nausea had gone away.

Mary and I stood up from the kneeler, and when we turned around we bumped into Edie, who lived downstairs from me. Edie drank tall cans of beer at her kitchen window, all by herself, directly facing no one on the other side of her table. She was always waiting, it seemed, for the chance to catch one of the neighborhood "little bastards" who came by like clockwork to bounce balls off the window where she sat. They threw all kinds of balls: super balls, tennis balls, wiffle balls, basketballs, knowing that it would send Edie into a shitfit, roaring and hollering and calling them every kind of a son of a bitch in the book. As time went on and kids began actually to hate Edie more and more — not just wanting a rise out of her — they threw the balls harder, breaking screens and glass. Before long there was a collection of balls on Edie's kitchen table. And there she continued to sit, in the same window, facing directly across from no one, never budging and never once entertaining the thought of sipping her beer on the couch across the room. After my brothers' deaths, I could sit in our third-floor window for hours, watching Edie in her second-floor window, wondering at her calling in life, and at my own. Now I was shocked to see Edie outside her apartment, never mind at George Fox's wake!

She told me he was her buddy. "And what are *you* doing here?" she asked me, looking me up and down as if I were on *her* turf, her after-hours world outside Old Colony. I told her I was his son, and she conceded, "Oh yeah, I'd say there's a resemblance," leaning back and studying my face a bit. She said he was a good guy, "a gem." Then she walked up to the casket, kissed her hand and laid it on her dead drinking buddy's forehead, and was out the door in a jiffy.

"I don't know. I guess he drank," Mary said, throwing up her hands. Then she peered back at his corpse again, from across the room, looking as if she wanted to go back, to check the broken blood vessels or some other signature of alcohol.

We took seats next to strangers who settled into an audible hush when they saw me. I started to notice quite a few glances at me from different parts of the parlor. One woman in particular seemed to be moving from one clique to another, telling people to take a look at me. I figured she knew who I was, and it actually felt good to be acknowledged, even in gossip. I thought I'd at least wait for my aunt Eileen — George's sister — so that we could thank her for her invitation and make a quick exit. I'd thought it was pretty generous of her to have gone out of her way to find my number and ask me to my father's wake. She'd said it was only right that I should attend, and I guess it was. The smell of carnations filled the air, and took me back to all those other wakes: ones for people I knew and cared for, like my brothers.

I guess I was still hoping for something maybe beyond — or better than — what I had known in the gangster-controlled Old Colony Project, where I'd seen family and neighbors die from violence and addictions. I hated being "white trash," and I was hoping that maybe I wasn't, or that half of me wasn't. I wanted to find something familiar at George's wake, something recognizable, but something that would make my most private dreams make sense. I hated being from racist, backward Southie, living among people who talked about niggers, drank a lot, buried their teenagers, and abided by the rules of their neighborhood drug lord, Whitey Bulger. I hated being poor. I hated being trash. I wasn't supposed to dream of anything more, so maybe I thought that if I discovered that half of me was from something a bit more sensible, more "normal," as Mary called it, then I'd be allowed to dream, to write stories, to make art, to eat strange food, to travel to places like Paris or just Cambridge, Massachusetts, and even to belong in such places outside Old Colony. I knew that there was something else that I had to have come from. My father did, after all, have a "big job" at the navy yard, whatever that was.

Mary stood up to look at the corpse again, and I just sat, somewhat anxious about Eileen Fox. I had met her only once, when she showed up at my brother Frankie's wake and introduced herself to me as my aunt, expressed her sympathies, and left. Frankie's wake was still a blurry memory, and I couldn't recall what Eileen had looked like. She'd brought her daughter Julie, my cousin, who I only remembered because she looked like me, in a dress. But the fact that they showed up, unlike my father, meant so much to me. Eileen sounded smart on the phone too, inviting me to George's wake, pronouncing her *r*'s and referring to our ancestors from Ireland: Foxes, Plunketts, and Cavanaughs, who she claimed were some very dignified people. She didn't know much about them except that they were some very dignified people, and that was good enough for me.

Mary sat again, looking distraught by her investigation into the life and death of George Fox. When I asked her what Eileen looked like, so I'd know her when she arrived, she told me that Eileen would be pretty except that she had a rotten angry face, kind of like someone who spent a lifetime sucking a lemon. Mary said she used to come screaming and hollering into Columbia Point Project to fight with her mother, Gertie, next door to us. She said everyone was afraid of her. I knew my mother hated Eileen too, but I figured she must have changed. After all, I had just talked to her on the phone the night before, when she called me to tell me that my father had died, that it was only right that I

should attend his wake, and that we came from some very dignified blood in counties Meathe and Cavan. She even invited me to
come visit her at her house in the suburbs and meet her daughters,
my cousins, who she bragged looked like Christie Brinkley.

A flutter of activity erupted at the door to the funeral parlor,
and Mary nudged me, looking scared. Eileen Fox looked dis-
tressed as she waved all the gathering well-wishers away from her.
She was well dressed, and seemed well mannered. Her daughter
Julie stood next to her, and lit up with recognition when she saw
me approach. But then she seemed to stop herself. I put my hand
out to greet Eileen, my aunt. She put her hand out in what looked
to me like a most dignified motion, and I noticed how well kept
her hands were, all manicured and decorated in gold jewelry.
Someone took the fur coat off her shoulders, and Eileen's hand
held mine. Her hand was warm and comforting.

"I wanted to thank you for inviting me," I said to Eileen.

"Who are you?" she asked, doing a double-take.

"Michael," I answered, "your nephew, George's son."

"My brother never had a son," she said, pulling her hand away
and turning her back to me quickly.

She approached the casket and made the sign of the cross.

The whole drive back to Old Colony Project I thought I might
be insane. Thank God Mary had witnessed the interaction with
Eileen, otherwise I might not have believed it had really happened. After all, it had been a strange few years of deaths and burials and disillusions, followed by more deaths and burials. I kept re-
playing it in my head: me being denied by the bitch who looked
like she'd spent a lifetime sucking a lemon, and her daughter who
looked like me, football player build and all. *Why would someone,
your aunt, invite you to your father's wake and then pretend she'd never
called you and tell you that your father is not your father?*

On my tenth birthday, while home alone and minding my baby
brother Seamus, I had looked up George Fox's mother in the

telephone book. I knew from Ma that he had lived with her in Dorchester. I had spent a whole morning getting up the guts to call, and when I did, Gertie answered with a cranky voice. I asked to speak to George. I told her that I was his son Michael and that she was my grandmother, as if we'd all be in for some kind of happy family reunion. "He doesn't have a son!" She yelled so loud I had to pull the telephone away from my ear. "Who put you up to this," she said, "your mother?" I told her my mother wasn't even home, and that I'd just called because it was my birthday — hoping now that I might get some kindness, as mention of birthdays usually did. That's when a man's voice came on the phone. "Michael?" It was the first time I'd ever heard my father's voice. I told him it was my birthday. "Who put you up to this, your mother?" I hung up the phone and went back to minding Seamus.

That was the only time I ever heard George Fox's voice, and every detail of his tone stuck with me to this day, nine years later. I wished I had never made that call. I wished I had never gone to his wake. Mary dropped me off in the project, and I went to my room and threw open the windows, letting out the day's pent-up heat and cockroach fumigation. Nighttime's whistles and hollers up to windows filled my room. Project nightlife. Family fights, teenage couples' shouts of "cocksucker" and "cunt" set to a background of blaring dance music, all made me hate my neighborhood, my family, myself. When the room cooled off, I lay on my mattress and wondered whether my aunt Eileen, like George and his mother, Gertie, just wanted nothing to do with someone like me.

Ma came into my room and asked me how the wake was. I told her about Eileen and how she'd acted. I told her I could have sworn she'd called me the day before, inviting me to my father's wake. "Oh," Ma said, shaking her head at Eileen's cunning, "she always was a cute bitch." "Huh?" I didn't know what Ma was getting at. All I knew was that I was late to the funeral of my father and that it was too late anyway ever to make up for how I'd never gotten to know him. "That cocksucker," Ma said. Now Ma's swears were only reminding me of how wretched our lives were, and how it was no wonder Eileen would deny the likes of me.

"Don't you see?" Ma said. "He must have left money! Eileen must have found out *after* she'd already called you, and then had to deny you, since you would be the next of kin." Ma reminded me that George was not on my birth certificate, since she hadn't been married to him. She'd given me Dave MacDonald's name, like all the other kids.

I was proud of Ma's detective work. I was determined now to show my face to Eileen Fox one more time. For once in my life I felt I should be proud of where I came from, who I was, and who I might become, and for a moment I was ashamed for having ever felt otherwise. I was pissed to think money could make someone change like that. I got Mary to drive me to the funeral. We went to the funeral parlor first, to see the body one last time, as families are invited to do. They closed the casket, though, as soon as I came into the room. I went to the funeral mass, and afterward I walked down the steps of the church behind Eileen and Julie, who by now was well trained not to acknowledge me. When I walked by the black limousine reserved for family, I stopped to look in. Eileen called out to a gang of George's drinking buddies who had no cars, and they all piled in, telling more stories of days and nights at the Emerald Isle. Eileen caught my eyes by accident, looked away, and then slammed the door shut.

Mary had to get to work at Boston City Hospital, and I was going to take the train home, but after Eileen's limo took off, I suddenly found myself surrounded by cousins and aunts of George Fox's, telling me they knew who I was and offering me a lift to the cemetery. I called Ma to tell her I was going to the cemetery, and she told me that she had done some more investigating and found that George had left about $75,000 between his savings and his life insurance policy. It pissed me off to think he had even a dime. I took a lift from the woman who, the evening before, had been alerting different cliques at the funeral parlor to my identity. She was George's cousin Louise, who said George hadn't talked to Eileen in years, and that he hated her. Louise said she'd always known about me, because George had taken me to her house when I was an infant, wanting her to help him shop for baby clothes. She said she'd wondered if I'd be at the wake, and that when she first laid eyes on me it was like seeing George Fox back from the dead, and I was even more like his brother Jimmy, the heroin addict who'd died just a few years earlier.

When we got to the cemetery I was greeted by a woman who had been George Fox's fiancée for ten years. She said that all of her family was staring at me in the church, and that her own son from a previous marriage said, "Who is he? He even walks like him!"

It felt good to be acknowledged. But I'd never had to think about my walk before now. And trudging over the spongy cemetery grass and mud toward a stranger's burial, I wondered at how someone could walk like a man he never knew.

MARY MORRIS

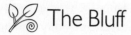 The Bluff

When I was a girl, growing up in Illinois, there was a bluff at the end of my block. It soared some three hundred feet above Lake Michigan and had a foot trail that ran along it. We'd moved to my town on the North Shore before many houses were built along that bluff, when it was still woods and meadows and one could follow these trails. I learned in my third grade that the Potawatomi had blazed them a century before.

I spent my days roaming these trails with my dogs. I was a pioneer girl, an Indian squaw. I was scanning the lake for canoes, braves coming home from the hunt. Or I was a lone pioneer woman, awaiting her husband's return from Fort Dearborn in the settlement the Indians called Chikagou, after the wild garlic that grew along its shores.

At the top of the bluff near the end of my street there was a tree that bent back into a curve. It had been bent this way by the strong winds off the lake and it never grew up straight. I liked to rest my back into its arch and stare out across the lake. For years I was a perfect fit. From there I gazed down at the roiling lake. I'd look out across the horizon and see as far as I could see.

Later, as I grew older, this was my favorite spot to go with a boy I liked. We could lean against this tree, the lake crashing below us, a strong wind pressing us close. At times we kissed, but they were the kisses of twelve-year-olds, and I never gave much thought to these secret yearnings as I nestled against a tree trunk high above the lake.

Then in the spring of eighth grade there were whisperings around school and we heard that Cindy Michaels, a girl from the other side of the tracks, had gotten caught having boys at her house. But not just having the boys over, because the boys had talked. They poked fun at her in the halls. They had done things to her. Unspeakable things we could barely imagine. And not just one boy but several. Whatever they had done, they talked about it. She was a locker-room joke.

Soon the girls knew about it. We'd heard. "Do you think it's true?" we asked as we walked to and from school. "Did they really do that to her?" Or, worse, did she do that to them? We had no idea what *that* really was, but we knew it was horrible. And then Miss Grunska called the girls for a meeting. I remember sitting in the back and Cindy Michaels and her mother up front.

Cindy was a big, bony girl, but her mother had long pale arms, a kind of reddish color, and reddish blond hair, frizzy, ratted on her head. She wore a white blouse, and I remember thinking that she had dressed especially for this occasion. She was a tall, slender woman and Cindy did not resemble her that much, though they both looked like people who had not had an easy life.

First Miss Grunska stood up. She was a round woman who wore long-sleeved gray wool dresses even on warm days, one of those schoolmarms who never married and had bad breath. She was our English teacher. And she began to talk to us about good girls and bad girls and how sometimes good girls do bad things. How a girl's reputation is all she has and she can ruin it in a heartbeat.

I remember wondering why the boys weren't getting the same lecture we were. Why they weren't being asked to bring in their parents and sit in front of the classroom as examples to the other boys. As Miss Grunska droned on, I tried to focus on what she was saying, but my mind wandered, because I wondered what the boys were doing and it was a hot spring day and the room smelled of dead fish.

Then suddenly Miss Grunska ordered Cindy Michaels to

stand up and make her confession. To tell us what the boys did to her and how sorry she was and how she wouldn't do it again. How she had been bad and been a bad example. That she had learned her lesson and now would be good.

I watched as our classmate rose for her public confession and apology. She wore a blue button-down shirt, neatly ironed, and her hair was curled. The wide bones of her face were grim and taut. As she began to speak, her face shattered into a million pieces like a plate glass window, and then she began to sob.

After school I walked to the bluff, to my place against the tree, where the tree was bent back in the wind. Leaning there, I smelled the dead fish. And then I saw them. There were miles of them, and they lined the beaches and shores. A million dead alewives, their insides sucked out by the lamprey eels that had invaded the Great Lakes. There would be no swimming all summer.

Leaning into the tree, the smell of dead fish all around, I knew that if I ever got into trouble, I would come to this place above the lake — a place I have always loved — and I would fling myself down.

My father had a standing bridge game every Saturday afternoon, and once every month or so the players met at our house. Eight men came and took over the den and living room with their card tables and cigars and corned beef sandwiches. Some of these men, such as Patrick Hennessey, were fathers of friends of mine, the girls I walked to school with.

I had to tiptoe around them. "Stay out of the way," my mother put it. Sometimes I was brought in for display. To say hello and be reminded of what a good student I was and how I should be a good girl. Some of the men asked me questions, such as if I enjoyed field hockey and had we gotten to the biology lesson where we had to pith the frogs. I liked these men, and Patrick Hennessey, who had a ruddy face and seemed to drink a lot, was among them. But mostly the men kept their heads down, faces in their cards, grunting hello, then turning back to their bridge partners and asking about some play that had just occurred.

There seemed to be this dark, clubbish world of men where women weren't allowed. A world of cigars and pumpernickel bread and gruff talk. And I knew that women could get in trouble and men would never be blamed.

I began to see boys. Some came to the door and introduced themselves to my parents, then took me to a movie or bowling with their father waiting in a car, then brought us home. But others I saw on the sly — at the deli after school, in the high school parking lot. There was Joe Rodriguez, and I'd slide down my drainpipe (I really could do this) to sneak out with him. And Jerry Nolan, the adopted boy from California who had returned to live with his father. Jerry had had some trouble out west and his father had called him home. He had a complicated, sad history, but he was a beautiful boy, though I've heard he has done little with his life.

I sneaked down the street to make out with Jerry on his couch in front of the TV. The blue light illumined our faces as we snuggled and kissed, sometimes rolling off his father's couch. And there were those dancing parties on Phyllis's sun porch, where we danced to Johnny Mathis singing "Small World" until some parent showed up and flicked on the lights.

And there was Bob Kee. The boy who met me a half-hour before my piano class and we'd kiss in a lonely stairwell until I had to run breathlessly up the stairs, always a little late, and play Chopin preludes for Mr. Heiselman.

Of course I wasn't anywhere near getting in trouble at this point. And though it was only kissing and for many, many years would not progress beyond this, I also knew it could and possibly would, and if anything happened to me, there was always the bluff.

I wasn't kidding about my plan. It was a pact I made with myself. Even as a young girl on walks along its trails, I had envisioned tormented squaws forced to marry old chieftains they did not love or pioneer women, widowed and alone in winter, flinging themselves down to the shore below.

I started to think of myself as someone who could get into trouble, and I knew from eighth grade that the boys would not be punished. I had glimpsed the dark world of men with their cigars and decks of cards. If I ever did get into trouble, jumping off this bluff, just at the end of my street, was preferable to having to tell my father. And I began thinking of the bluff as the place of my demise.

✿

In high school there were cars. And there were boys who had cars and we drove around. We went to McDonald's, then drove around the cornfields. But mostly we'd drive down to the lake and hope that the police had just made their rounds. Then we could kiss and hold one another and sometimes do more.

There were girls who did get into trouble during those years. I'd seen girls who'd grown fat be sent away for three or four months, then return home thin and sad. One girl got a big potbelly that showed in her blue gym suit and then she was gone until the next year. We were told she had the flu. It was never talked about, really, where they'd gone. It was an odd disappearing act girls could do back then.

✿

When I was sixteen and in love with a boy named Sean and the bluff seemed more as if it could become a reality, my girlfriend Lorna, whose father was Patrick Hennessey, was kicked out of her home. I found her sobbing on the street corner one morning as we picked her up for school. She told us she was "in trouble" and her father had told her to get the hell out. "Where am I going to go?" she said. She was told to pack her bags and be gone by the end of the week, to go live with "that trash" who'd gotten her this way in the first place.

She cried and cried and said her father was a drunk and he hit her, and she showed us a red mark on her face. But it didn't seem to matter to her so much that he'd hit her. What mattered was that she'd been thrown out of her home.

The following Saturday my father's bridge game was at my house. I'd said nothing to my father about what was going to happen to Lorna Hennessey, but I could tell the mood over cards was dark and tense. No one seemed much in the game. No one said, "Howya doing, Maryoutchie," or whatever they called me when I brought them a tray of pastrami sandwiches. They didn't ask how field hockey was going. They kept their heads down on the cards, once in a while shouting at one another.

Then the game was over and everyone went home, including Patrick Hennessey, who stumbled out, his face red from drinking. Afterward, walking by the den, I picked up the phone to make a call and heard my father on the line. He was talking to a man who was shouting at him and my father was shouting back. Perhaps because they were yelling at one another, they didn't hear me on the line.

"I'm telling you, Patrick," my father said, "you are making a mistake with this girl."

"Mind your own business. It's not your daughter," Patrick Hennessey said. I had my ear so tightly against the receiver it hurt, and I was holding my breath.

"Well, I can tell you one thing. If Mary got into trouble, the one place she could come would be home." I closed my eyes, then gently cradled the receiver.

That afternoon I went with my dogs for a walk to the bluff. It was a spring day, but the wind off the lake was still cutting cold. I didn't mind. I tucked my back against the tree and stood there. I rested my back into the curve of the tree and stayed for a very long time.

BICH MINH NGUYEN

 Toadstools

We live in a neighborhood of Vanderveens and Hoekstras, with ranch houses, Sears siding, and rec room basements. My sister and I have tagged two houses as "rich": the blue split-level on the corner with a wide sloping lawn and the one with the swimming pool. It's a real pool, not one of those aboveground tubs covered with a tarp. In the summer that in-ground pool glistens as pure and fenced and untouchable as the old white couple who own it. They invite no one but our next-door neighbors, and from a distance we imagine their pale heads shining wet; we hear the splashes they make while we run through the sprinklers in our back yard.

My grandmother's voice rises above all others in the neighborhood, calling my siblings and me home for lunch. Every day we have feasts: bowls of pho, stewed shrimp with rice. Homemade french fries are nestled under garlic-seared minute steaks. One day I bring over a friend so she can get in on the action too. But my friend shrinks back. She takes a couple of fries and refuses anything more. She shakes her head, blond curls quivering. She says, "Your house smells funny."

And like that my world divides in half. Outside I climb trees, ride bicycles around the block, chase down ice cream trucks with the girls in the neighborhood. We are friends in certain hours, the interstices between our real lives. When they go off for Vacation Bible School I go back home, where our driveway is patchy with motor oil. There are junk drawers, junk cabinets, a junk garage. In the kitchen Noi is opening cans of lychee and serving the fruit in teacups; she carves apples and mangoes clean of skin. She spends her days knitting sweaters and blankets, reading up on the news from Vietnam, working in the kitchen. When she tunes in to *Another World* and a language she doesn't understand I sit beside her, reading library books that pile around me and never get returned on time.

On the weekends my family goes to the Saigon Market, where the shelves are crammed with rice paper and tea. My father spends hours talking to the storeowner; they go over business, relatives, the latest ones to arrive. He buys my sister and me bags of dried cuttlefish and plums, and we go outside to look in the windows of the Waterbed Gallery next door. There's always broken glass in the parking lot, and we wonder where it comes from. On 28th Street all the cars are going fast, headlights winking on toward darkness. Sometimes we're allowed to walk to Meijer's and buy an orange crush. The fluorescent aisles hold stories of other people's houses: Hamburger Helper, Shake 'n' Bake, gravies made by Knorr; meatloaves, casseroles, pork chops with applesauce.

Before falling asleep at night I go to Noi's room and ask for permission. *Grandmother, good night; may I go to sleep now?* She sits cross-legged, working on a puzzle, and sometimes her long silver hair is down, pooled around her like a cape. She might let me go with a wave of her hand. She might say no, so I'll stay and have an apple. Once in a while I help with a puzzle; I sit beside her and read the same books to stamp them in my mind. There are times I return again and again, barging in on her late-night meditations to ask the same question until my parents yell at me to be quiet and go to bed.

The truth is that the neighborhood has been going downhill. Our next-door neighbors can no longer ignore the silent man who lives alone and never mows his lawn. They move carefully past the divorced woman — absent ex-husband never mentioned — who lives with her two kids and a deaf cat. They speak in frightened whispers about the "hyper" boy down the street. My family's arrival has signaled a turning point. We are a pieced-together lot, not white, not Republican, not Christian. My stepmother is Latina and has declined to change her last name; my father works shirtless in the yard. My stepsister has been caught smoking; my sister has threatened to beat up a girl who made fun of her clothes. My brother leads big-wheel parades around the block; my uncles blast Santana from the basement. And I am always lurking, making up gossip. We are funny-looking. Funny-smelling. Our souls are not saved.

And on days after rain when toadstools bloom in our yard my grandmother goes out and digs up each one. The kids in the neighborhood see this and screw up their faces. "Are you gonna eat them for supper?" they call out, laughing, their Kool-Aid mouths wide.

It takes me years to understand what Noi is doing. The realization begins on the night of a school play in sixth grade. Everyone will go except my grandmother, who has decided that her presence would be an embarrassment. She wouldn't wear her *ao dai* and endure my eyes cast downward. So we leave for the play and I am bothered the whole time. I want to go back and tell her that I never meant to be ashamed of us; I never meant to absorb that point of view. I want to say so much, but I do not.

So I say this now: I know why she dug up the toadstools. Here is a woman with an imagination, who supplies her own meanings to soap operas she doesn't really comprehend. I think she must have pictured my siblings and me stealing away with the toadstools, putting their foreign substance in our mouths. She never acknowledged the neighborhood children laughing, their cheeks puffed with derision. When she knelt in the yard she pulled up the toadstools to save us.

We owe our childhoods to other people. In 1975 my father and grandmother gathered up their family and fled from Vietnam to start over on the other side of the world. I wonder what Noi must have thought that first winter in Michigan. The breathless cold, falling ice, drifts of snow so high months would pass before we'd see the yard again. From her bedroom window the streetlamps cast an eerie glow on the neighborhood. I wonder now when I stopped asking her for permission. How many nights did I return, lonely and wide awake, saying *Grandmother, may I go to sleep now?*

HOWARD NORMAN

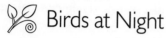 Birds at Night

FOR EMMA

There is Happiness, which passes in a vague state, an inkling, a shadow, an echo through one's memory, whereas Sadness is an adhesive — memories cling to it. (During the flute solo, the eye is still drawn to the silent cello.)

There are some writers and readers for whom only the tangible, calculable, verifiable, factual can truly credit and serve recollection. (Indeed, certain radio talk-show hosts seem able to comprehend a novel only via the question "Which parts are actually true?") This attitude persists at the expense of art, intensifying the denigration of wholly imaged novels or short stories, even a "memoir" that contains revised or reconfigured personal history for the sake of verisimilitude.

Here are a few facts of my childhood:

I was mostly raised in Grand Rapids, Michigan. In the summer of 1965, I worked in a bookmobile. The driver's name was Pinnie Olen. I was sixteen that previous March. For working in the bookmobile, I was paid sixty cents an hour and worked forty-four hours per week. I got to keep ten dollars per week; the rest went to my mother, Estelle, which was fine with me. "You're supporting me," is how she put it, "as your father's mostly out of the picture."

These are facts, but then there are the emotional dimensions of childhood and young adulthood, more difficult to calibrate, more rewarding to ponder, and which contain more gravitas than does any merely factual testimony that one lived and felt things deeply.

So when I add that I can truly recall only one conversation with my father with any confident degree of accuracy, I mean it. He had been away for about a year. My mother said he lived in California, but I saw him in Grand Rapids two or three times through the window of the bookmobile, and said nothing, because I didn't want to embarrass my mother. He was living across town, which explains how he heard on WORD AM radio that I had won $666 in a contest. I had not entered it; the station had put the license plate numbers of thousands of cars in a hopper and the morning DJ, Marty Sobieski — "Mad Marty" — had reached in and plucked out mine. When on a morning in late July I heard my license plate number on the radio, I telephoned right in. On the air, Mad Marty said, "Well, Howard Norman, of 1727 Giddings Street, get on down to the station and we'll cut you a check, and you can ask the girl of your dreams out to dinner!" Then he played "Sherry," an incredibly popular hit by the Four Seasons and an homage to the falsetto voice. I had only a month earlier obtained my legal driver's license. However, I had been driving a claptrap 1962 Chevrolet for over a year; the street map of Grand Rapids was a grid of illegal sojourns. My older brother had sold me the car. It turned out that he had heard me win the contest from his cell at the Kent County Correctional Facility, where he was serving thirty days for breaking and entering.

Except for Division, Cherry, and Giddings Streets, I cannot recall the names of streets, but can recall pulling the Chevrolet into the A&E Drive-In, with its individual speakerphones on poles, and waiting for Karen Eldersveld, my self-proclaimed love interest, to roller-skate out and take my order. Her father was a policeman. Every time I ordered a root beer and hot dog, or chili dog, she would say, "You're not supposed to be driving. You wouldn't want me to tell my dad, would ya?" Enunciated with slow charm (she was busy, no time to repeat herself), this was her standard bribe for an outsized tip. Clipped to my belt was one of those press-down change dispensers with individual metal silos for nickels, dimes, and quarters, the kind that people hawking magazines and cabdrivers had. I always left Karen the painfully extravagant amount of a dollar tip. One night, six months before I had my license, her father pulled his police cruiser up directly next to my car. He looked over, registering my face and countenance, until Karen skated up and said, loud enough for me to hear, "Hi, Pop — hey, look, that's Howard Norman in that car. He's a year ahead of me at Ottawa Hills. He supports his mother." Her father reappraised me with a somber, sympathetic look and nodded. After he got his hot dog and cup of coffee, he backed the cruiser slowly out of the parking lot. Almost immediately Karen skated up and said, "For the 'grade older' part, that'll be two dollars, please." I always thought of her as a good businesswoman.

Thus I mostly learned Grand Rapids at night. Though it was a growing city, my rounds, if you will, comprised stopping at places not especially associated with urban life. I had a precise, unwavering chronology. First I would park near the faux Mississippi steamboat at Reeds Lake and look at seagulls. Summer gulls always attended the steamboat, having migrated in from Lake Michigan. At night they roosted along the chipped railings, deck chairs, calliope pipes. They flew in and out of the shadows. Sometimes the weight of three or four dozen gulls noticeably moved the paddle wheel.

From the steamboat I would drive to the Thornapple River and park at the least popular spot in the quintessential make-out lot, where one stifling hot night I saw my brother's Studebaker with its windows down. His radio was playing. The area for some reason was marked by a white picket fence. You could hear the river from your car. Anyway, I studied my brother's car from a distance. At one point, with an exacting moment of help from moonlight, I saw a pair of feet atop the front seat — red shoes still on — and marveled at the geometric inventiveness of lovemaking in a car seat. "Sherrr-eee, Sherry bay-bee, can you come out tonight? Come, come, come out to-niiight."

Navigating past love cars, I would work my way down a steep path to the riverbank. There I would shine my flashlight on the surface, hoping to lure the ghoulish, whiskered face of a catfish. (There was a rumor when I was a kid that catfish had a kind of electrical circuitry, and if you got cut by a catfish's razor lips, a terrible shock befell you.) Mostly, however, I shined the light out onto the river for ducks, geese, the occasional loon; water birds were active at night more often than people knew.

Next I would drive about a mile upriver to the elevated osprey's nest, on a pole about ten yards out into the river. Looking back on it, I realize that this setup was an early example of ecological protection; on shore was a sign warning that any damage to the roost or the ospreys themselves led to a $1,000 fine. One night I saw an osprey glide in to the roost, and its body seemed illuminated from within, like a lampshade, though of course it was the effects of the moon. The osprey had a fish in its beak. I remember saying the word *magic* out loud, feeling embarrassed right away, even though I was alone. However, if magic is a conjunction of rare, disparate, and vivid elements, the sight of that osprey with pale moonlight igniting its chest feathers and wings qualified as magic.

Last I would drive to see the swans at Ebbets Lake, which, in every dimension, was a subsidiary of Reeds Lake, but the place the swans preferred.

This, then, was my nocturnal gazetteer of bird life, and is what I remember with the most permanent affection.

So birds provided a kind of aesthetic sustenance, and pleasing memories. One Saturday morning in early August, I happened to be looking out of my second-floor bedroom window at the very moment my father drove up and parked in the driveway. I remember thinking, "Where'd he get that car?" He had left driving a Ford and now returned driving a Pontiac. He stepped from the car, looked at the side door a moment, walked to the back of the car, popped the trunk, reached in, took out a ball-peen hammer, closed the trunk, flattened his left hand against the sloping part of the trunk, took a deep breath, then slammed the hammer against his left hand, purposely, it looked to me, striking his thumb. A wince of electric pain contorted his handsome face. Possibly because I had done well in geography that year in school and suddenly referred to it for desperate irony, the first thought I had was that the state of Michigan is shaped like a mittened hand, the thumb slightly extended. (People said, "I live in the thumb.")

I heard the side door open. My mother was at work taking care of children at the orthodox shul near downtown. My two younger brothers were at my aunt's. My older brother was out along some highway clearing weeds or putting down tar with the other juvenile delinquents, as they were called back then. I went downstairs to see my father.

I stood in the kitchen doorway. My father sat at the table. He looked over at me and said, "You're too skinny. You're a skinny goat, son."

"I'm your son. Does that make you a goat too?"

"Ha-ha and ha."

"Why'd you do that, Dad? To your thumb, there."

He held out his hand as if beholding some object entirely separate from him. "Oh, that," he said. "I accidentally slammed it in the car door. Get me some ice cubes and a towel, will you?"

But I stood my ground, staring at him. I was dressed (this is definitely accurate) in a black T-shirt and light green shorts, and I was barefoot. I was the only of my friends, in fact the only young man I knew, who had a ponytail.

"What's that on the back of your head?" my father said. My father was nothing if not well groomed. He was five feet eight, slim, with beautiful blue eyes, curly brown hair cut in what he called a "businessman's cut." What he did for a living I had not the slightest clue.

"Cat got your tongue?" he said. He walked to the Kelvinator refrigerator, opened the door, opened the small freezer door, took up a butter knife and chipped out the ice-cube tray, slammed the tray on the lip of the sink, pried up a few cubes, wrapped them in a dishtowel, then sat down at the table again. He swathed his thumb in the towel.

"Slammed it in a car door, huh?" I said.

"What's that on the back of your head?"

"Where's the hammer? Still in the trunk?"

"What hammer, exactly, are you referring to?"

We looked at each other a long, silent moment.

"I guess that's a badge of individuality, that ponytail, or is there something you want to tell me? Is there something you want to tell me?"

"Like what?"

"Such as you aren't the kind of young man interested in having a girlfriend. Something along those lines."

I could hear the refrigerator humming.

"If you've been living in California, how come you've got Michigan plates, Dad?"

"It's a borrowed car."

"Borrowed from who?"

"Someone you don't know. Someone you'll never know."

"What color is a California license plate anyway? I've never seen one."

"It's blue with a palm tree on it."

"That seems more like Florida."

"California copied the idea — how do I know? What's so important about it to you?"

"Nothing."

"Maybe you need money for a haircut. Maybe that hairdo's the result of financial restrictions around this house in my absence. Is that it? I could give you a haircut right now, just with the kitchen scissors."

"No thanks."

The ice cubes were melting out onto the table.

"Speaking of license plates . . . ," he said. He adjusted the towel and winced.

"What about them?"

"Let's reverse a situation here, shall we?"

"Whaddaya mean?"

"Let's reverse a situation. Say you dropped by my place of residence and said you were temporarily not flush. Do you think for one minute I'd hesitate to reach into my pocket, snap out my wallet, and hand you a roll of five-dollar bills, or tens, or twenties, peel off a few fifties for you? Right there on the spot."

"I'm sixteen, Dad. I work in the bookmobile. Maybe you didn't know that. Maybe that news didn't reach you in California. I'm never flush."

"Speaking of license plates, you're pretty flush now, aren't you?"

"You musta had the radio on in your borrowed car, huh?"

"Imagine how proud I felt, just flew into town and the first news I get is my boy's a millionaire."

"Imagine."

Then came the turning point in the conversation. I did not recognize it at the time, but it definitely was the turning point. I knew where things were heading now, that my father wanted my prize money. Right then and there I was fully resigned to it. But asking for the money was not the turning point.

My father sensed that it was exactly the moment to punch his right thumb with his left fist, and instead of loosing a howl of pain, he more or less threw his head back, crying out, "Sher-r-r-eee, Sher-ree ba-a-bee, Sherrr-eee, won't you come out to-night?" in a falsetto that would match Frankie Vallee's in pitch and intensity any day. He was forty-four years old at the time, nearly a decade younger than I am as I write this. He had quit smoking. He was living somewhere. Anyway, I cracked up laughing to think of him listening to the Four Seasons on the AM rock-and-roll station.

It was some connection, at least.

And he further seized the moment. "Hey — I could drive you

over to the Old Kent Bank and cash your check, or be right there when you cashed it. Did you cash it already?"

"No, it's upstairs."

"I'd've thought your mother might've cashed it."

"No."

"Well, you don't need an adult to go with you. Not at age sixteen. But I'd volunteer."

"Where've you been all this past year, anyway?"

"Mostly California."

"Sure."

"Mostly."

"What happened, Dad, all the support checks get lost in the mail?"

"You know how I feel about the postal system."

"Yeah, well, Mom's not exactly flush."

"Whoa, now, son. Hold on. Hold on, there. The adult finances — now that's not your business. That's not —"

"I'll give you a hundred dollars."

"How about half? How about a two-way split, three thirty-three?"

"I'll give you a hundred dollars. How long are you here? You going to see Mom?"

"Actually, your mother doesn't know I came over today."

"Dropped in from California."

"No need to tell her, really. Now that our business transaction is completed. It's a loan, mind you."

"I'll get my shoes on."

"Old Kent Bank's open till noon Saturdays, I noticed."

"I'm giving the rest to Mom."

"Well, maybe keep some for yourself, kid. You won it fair and square. It was your license plate, wasn't it."

"I'll do what I want."

"Fine, do what you want."

"Nice to agree with so disagreeable a person, as Mom would say."

"Oh, she says that, does she?"

"Yes."

"Look at this mess, ice cubes melting all over the place, and what kind of son do I have, merely a smidgen of sympathy for a man who slammed his thumb in a car door. There's pain involved in that."

(Enough sympathy to obtain a hundred dollars, I later thought. But that was my fault. He was just practicing his craft. He was working the room, and I happened to be the only other person in it.)

"We could stop at Blodgett Memorial. They could look at your thumb."

"No, no — life's generally an emergency, isn't it, but this thumb's not."

"I don't know what you mean."

"Let's drop it. Let's drop the subject. The bookmobile, that's your summer job, I take it."

"Yes."

"What's your wages?"

"Six hundred sixty-six dollars an hour, Dad. That's what I'm paid. Since you asked. Since you're so interested. I file cards in the card catalog. I dust the books. I fill out overdue notices. I do everything there is to do. You used to read books. You should drop in there, find a book."

"I've got to get back to California, truth be told. So just imagine how overdue that book would be, huh?"

We drove to the Old Kent Bank. I cashed the check. The teller had heard the contest on the radio and commented on my luck. While still in the bank I handed my father ten ten-dollar bills. There was no more bargaining or conniving. "I'll walk home, thanks," I said.

In the parking lot, he said, "Yes, it's a nice day for a walk. A nice summer's day to be sixteen, out walking."

"Okay, then, Dad, see ya."

He slid into his car and drove off. I noticed that he adjusted the

rearview mirror once I was out of its range. But then he screeched
the Pontiac into a U-turn and stopped next to me. He stretched
his arm out the window. "Men shake hands when they part company after a business deal," he said. We shook hands. He drove off
again. I had $566 in my back pocket. I walked directly to the Buy
Right, a drugstore, where I purchased a notebook and pen. I sat on
the bus waiting bench out front and wrote down the conversation
I had just had with my father; even in that amount of time there
may have inadvertently been emendations, a sculpted sentence or
two, an added word for emphasis in immediate retrospect. Anyway, I wrote things down. I kept the "dialogue" for thirty-seven
years; surely it registered one of the earliest moments, perhaps unbeknown to me, when writing became something.

When my mother came home from work, she said, "I'm beat."
I had already cleaned up the kitchen spick-and-span. I handed
her the $566. She counted it out on the kitchen table and said,
"Whew, that's some cash, huh? So, what? You kept a hundred dollars for yourself. That's a lot of money, sweetheart. Use it in good
health, okay? It's only fair. Well, one way or the other, it all goes
for household upkeep, doesn't it? I'm going to have a lemonade,
then go over and pick up your brothers. Want to come with?"

That night, again, as I would most every night that summer, I
toured the bird haunts and was quite successful, seeing what I had
come to see.

 The Gravedigger's Daughter

Run, run! Run to your hiding place beneath the bridge.

You are ten years old. You are running from your father's up-raised fist. Though knowing he would never hit *you*.

Here, the echoing underside of the bridge over the canal at Drumm Road. Ghost faces reflected upward from the fast-moving water below.

That high-arched old iron bridge over the Erie Barge Canal on the outskirts of Ransomville, New York. That long-ago time of which no one now wishes to speak. Your hiding place beneath the bridge amid scum-encrusted rocks and boulders and crumbling concrete supports fouled with the birdlime of decades. Fifty years later you will remember the sharp stony odor, voices murmuring and quarreling in the water, and the deeper, pulsing silence of that place.

Ask why: Ask God why! Why such things are allowed.

Pappa's voice choked in fury and in shame.

That voice you'd rarely heard until now, except through a shut door, the walls of your parents' bedroom.

That voice that would lodge deep in you, that you would come to fear and to hate.

Your lost cousins. See!

In the shallow water near shore there are chunks of broken concrete from the bridge's construction, rusted pipes, metal rods protruding from the water like unwanted thoughts.

Beneath the bridge is a forbidden place for a child of ten. A dangerous place. You crouch panting between the gigantic rocks, on your heels that begin to ache with the strain. *Ask God why, why such things are allowed. Children sentenced to death . . .*

Your cousins are Elzbieta, Freyda, and Leon. In the photographs they are smiling shyly, frowning. Elzbieta is the eldest, and Freyda is the youngest, said to be your age. You are fascinated by Freyda — she has your eyes! Dark-shadowed eye sockets, a creased forehead unusual in one so young. You hold the photograph to the light with a childish desire to see more of her, as if the wrinkled stiff rectangle of paper were a way in to that other world where somehow the child Freyda Morgenstern is you.

Your mother plaits your hair into tight braids sometimes for school, the way Freyda's hair is plaited. Your hair is thick and curly and inclined to snarls like tiny spider's nests Momma scolds, and plaiting it tight until it hurts is a way of taming it.

Your cousins' last name is not your last name, for your name was changed at Ellis Island when your parents entered the United States just a few months before you were born. A long-ago time that frightens you to contemplate. When Rebecca did not exist, only your brothers existed to be brought to America. Your last name was trimmed and Americanized and is now easy to pronounce: not Morgenstern but Morgan — with an *a*, Pappa says, mocking. Like the dun-colored feathers of sparrows picking in the dirt, your family is camouflaged in a remote corner of upstate New York in a country town twenty miles from Lake Ontario.

Why sent back? A "quo-ta," they are claiming.

No more refugees, it means! No more Jews.

The fishermen's path beside the canal is narrow and choked with weeds. In places there is hardly any path at all. You run, stumbling dangerously close to the edge of the bank, where dry earth crumbles into the canal. If your mother could see you she would scream and grab at you, but your mother is too far away and will never follow you here.

Approaching a bridge from beneath, your eyes lift anxiously to the underside of the structure. You see rusted girders and ugly gi-

gantic screws and that look of the underside of things, like skele-
tons you are not meant to see nor even to imagine.

On days of bright sunshine you can be blinded by the shadow
beneath the bridge.

The canal at Drumm Road. The canal that flows through your
dreams.

It is said of the Erie Canal that it's deeper than it appears. In
the heat of August it looks as if you could walk on its surface:
opaque as lead.

Be good, Rebecca! My good girl who is all I have, I must trust you.

You have never known what your mother means by such
words. You have never been able to predict your mother's emotions, which change swiftly as the sky above Lake Ontario, which
is a clear washed blue one minute and the next minute mottled
with swollen thunderheads. Sometimes Momma digs her fingers
into your hair, draws in her breath *Oh! oh! oh!* as if she is drowning.
You run from Momma, who has been crying this morning, and
you run from Pappa, who raised his fist to you.

Beneath the bridge has been your hiding place since early summer. You are fascinated by the way the light reflects upward onto
the underside of the bridge, ghost faces that shimmer and fade as
you stare at them, then reappear in the corner of your eye when
you glance away. The swift-moving water casts up murmurous
voices of the kind you hear on the brink of sleep. You are frightened of copperhead snakes here, at the water's edge. Those spiders
that spin funnel webs like cotton candy. Your mother would be furious at you, squatting on your heels at the water's edge, sweaty
and panting like a dog. Clouds of gnats drift onto you like dreamy
thoughts sticking to your eyelashes and in your hair.

You lower your hand into the water. Always it's a surprise, the
water is so soft. Warm as tears. A caress, an invisible hand clasping
yours.

How would you like two sisters, Rebecca? Your cousins from far away.
One day Momma spoke gaily, like a drunken woman. Her eyes
shone damp with an emotion you could not decipher.

You hear: a vehicle approaching on Drumm Road. A flatbed truck driving fast along the road that in this long-ago time isn't yet paved but only strewn with coarse gravel. The bridge has been built high over the canal to allow the passing of barges, and so the road abruptly ascends a steep hill. The truck noisily changes gears and clatters onto the bridge, crossing not twelve feet above your head.

Bits of dirt fall like rain, the noise is deafening. The plank floor shudders as if it's about to collapse. Your instinct is to run away like a panicked rabbit but you crouch, hugging your knees to your chest. Such a skinny child you could squeeze beneath the big rocks like a snake, you could hide in the moist-sucking crevices beneath the rocks. Not breathing, you hold yourself still until the truck is past. And the pulsing murmurous silence of the canal returns.

And no one has seen you.

You, the gravedigger's daughter. Safe because no one has seen you.

&

You had not asked *Why?* of your father when he revealed the terrible news. Never do you or your brothers ask *Why?* of your father.

Like cattle sent back to Hitler! Nine hundred seventy-six refugees on that ship.

Cries of cicadas in the trees. Frantic to mate, and to die.

That late-summer smell of rotting things, so sweet.

On the bridge's underside, shifting parabolas of light.

Elzbieta, Freyda, Leon. They had become real to you and now they will become unreal. Ghost cousins. Their parents are your father's older brother and sister-in-law from your father's hometown, Kaufbeauren, south of Munich. They had fled the Nazis into Belgium, and into France, and finally into Portugal. They were passengers on an Italian ship called the *Marea* that embarked from Lisbon in July 1941 but was turned back by U.S. Immigration at New York harbor.

Ask why? Ask God why.

Ask the hypocrite Roosevelt.

Hide your eyes not to see your cousins' faces. Shut your ears not to hear your father's angry words.

Ask Him who casts the dice. Not me, who is no more than dice, the gravedigger. No more than a shadow passing over the face of the deep.

Momma pleaded with him not to tell you such things. His mouth damp with spittle, not to shout such things. *The child is too young, she doesn't need to know,* Momma said, but Pappa shoved her aside in a fury for you must never tell Pappa what to do. Shouting at her *Go away! Shut your mouth! She needs to know, she can't be a baby forever.*

Pappa's face is ugly, a fist of a face. His eyes are like gasoline before a match is tossed. Tears spill onto his cheeks you are not meant to see.

No child is meant to see the tears of her father.

You will come to think: Freyda was your age in the photograph, but when had the photograph been taken, and when had it been sent to your father in Ransomville? The letter hadn't come from Europe but from relatives in Brooklyn.

This time of confusion and displacement. Where the places you lived are not where you were born or meant to endure.

Hiding places, for some.

Marea, the ship was called. *Marea,* you whisper aloud beneath the bridge. A name of romance you will one day learn means *tide.*

Not a romantic name at all. Not a name of mystery. High tide, low tide. You shut your eyes and see God tossing His dice.

Why not kill them on the ship, set the ship on fire. A more merciful death than the cattle cars and the camps and the gas ovens.

When Pappa saw you cringing he raised his fist to you — not to hit, Pappa would never hit his daughter! — but to warn.

Go away, then. Get out of here. I don't want to see your face either.

Through the back yard you run. Through the overgrown part of the cemetery you run. As at school you are made to run, chased and jeered at by older children. *Gravedigger's daughter!*

Heart beating like a silly little bird trapped inside your chest.

One of those fluttery bright-yellow birds that live in the under-
brush along the canal.

Never would Pappa hit *you*. He has struck your brothers, and
he has struck your mother, but never *you*.

Rebecca, you are. Rebecca Morgan. Next month you will be in
fifth grade.

Not Freyda Morgenstern. Not her.

In the old country Pappa was a printer of scientific journals, in
the new country he is a cemetery groundskeeper. *Gravedigger!*
sniggering boys call in his wake.

Other words, too, are called. Pappa does not hear.

*In animal life the weak are quickly disposed of. So you must hide your
weakness. We must.*

His revenge is to mock. He mocks those people among whom
he dwells, camouflaged as a sparrow is camouflaged against the
dirt. He mocks the solemn engraved words on their grave mark-
ers. *Heaven! Jesus our Redeemer! Life everlasting! As if there is heaven
or hell except what humankind has created.*

You laugh when he laughs. Yet you fear his eyes.

Shiny eyes of gaiety, fury. Desperation.

You have come to hate the shabby stone house in the cemetery.
Smelling of kerosene, lye soap, fried fat. Smelling of damp black
earth and the rotting of corpses.

Beneath the bridge on this day in late summer you hide, you can
make yourself skinny as a snake to slip between the boulders. Another vehicle passes clattering overhead, another rain of dirt. Like
something melting the sun drifts downward in the sky, toward the
dense tree line. Your thoughts break and scatter like dragonflies
skittering on the surface of the water, and you sink into an uncomfortable, shallow sleep from which you wake trembling with hunger, not knowing at first where you are.

Rebecca? Rebecca —

MICHAEL PARKER

Movie Where You Don't See the Monster Until the End

We rode up to town. That lazy hour after supper, porch sitters, pickups crawling along the country road we lived on. Me and my little sister and my dad in my dad's old panel truck with the plywood box for a passenger's seat. My older sister, fourteen then, would not let my dad drop her off at the high school in what we called his work truck. This was 1971, and panel trucks and vans weren't yet cool, and nothing driven by your daddy, especially something that puffed cloudy black smoke thicker than the chemicals the mosquito man spread along his route in the bug-bad eastern North Carolina summer, was cool.

So my daddy would let her out and follow her a block to see that she made it, and my little sister and year-older brother and I, barely past kindergarten, would crowd on the box and watch her ignore us as she smoked the sidewalks left to school. There we were again, watching her ignore us all the way up to town, two miles in the dusky heat on an autumn evening when she had announced at supper she had somewhere to go and my dad said, No ma'am, you're staying right here, and my mother had the good sense to stay out of it as did both my brothers, but when my sister said Oh Yes I Sure Am and stood up, pushing the oldest-sibling-side of the table right up into the rib cages of us three youngest, who were crammed along a bench upside the stove island, when my sister pivoted around like she'd been trained to do in her halftime show and marched right out of the house and my father did not view myself as a child at all. I was incredibly sophisticated in my own head even as I was what people today call "prepubescent," not yet in my teens but just on the brink. And likewise, America was on the threshold of a whole new phase. People referred to that period as the Age of Aquarius.

Except it was really Chicago, circa 1969. Jupiter may have been aligned with Mars, but none of us knew it on the south side of the city, where we watched TV in black and white, played our forty-fives on a record player with a worn-down needle and a nickel balanced on the arm so the record wouldn't skip. We wore those records out, listening to Harold Melvin and the Blue Notes, Sam and Dave, and Wilson Pickett. We did the funky Broadway and the boogaloo and even the twist (though it was considered by then an "old" dance). We wore white bobby socks, high-top sneakers, knee-highs, and penny loafers. We curled our hair on weekends, sitting under the dryer at twelve years old. And smoked in the schoolyard, hours after school was out, puffing like crazy without inhaling, the cigarettes our props in our roles as would-be adolescents.

When we slow-danced, we wrapped our arms around our partner's neck and stepped in close, our head on his shoulder while Smokey Robinson and the Miracles crooned. We learned how to follow, even as we liked to lead, at blue-light parties in basements where parents left us to our own devices. We played "ashes," where you sat in a circle and passed a cigarette around, person to person, until the ash landed on someone, who then had to perform a truth or dare. Usually the dare involved going into the closet and kissing somebody. They were chaste kisses with nice boys as innocent as we were. But who still loved to slow-dance and hold you tight on the dance floor. We didn't drink alcohol and we didn't do drugs. But drugs were in the air, and we knew about them. Beatles songs alluded to them, and we deciphered their lyrics. "Norwegian Wood" was about marijuana. "Lucy in the Sky with Diamonds" was about LSD, or so we were told. A Tempta-

LISA PAGE
 Psychedelic Shack

Childhood is in a way a myth; we believe we grow out of it, shed it like an old skin. We buy into the notion that it is one section of our lives removed from the rest. We idealize it, believing its magic superior, thinking once we were little, but now we are not. The truth is, our bodies change throughout our lives. We don't just "grow up," we grow older, and the idea of innocence can seem like an alien concept. But the child remains, transcended, often denied, but there all the same, hiding beneath our business suits, our corporate uniforms, the camouflage we wear to communicate our grown-up selves. We are no longer children in a physical way. But we retain the essence of it in our secret dreams and aspirations. We are still gullible, silly, naughty, and full of ourselves. We do not eschew our childhoods and subsist only as adults, because the whole experience is seamless, even as we like to break it into smaller portions, believing things are easier that way. We are who we are early on. And even as we mature, we digress. We shed not one skin but many. We grow older, we get "better." And the real essence of childhood is something we reach for and sometimes attain. We view our innocence with new eyes and appreciate it. To paraphrase the old song, we understand that we were so much older then — we're younger than that now! Even as, technically, the opposite is true.

The apex of my childhood was in the 1960s. I say apex because the world felt wide open then in a way it has never felt since. But I

Barely can you hear your mother calling you. Yet you've been hearing, in your sleep.

Here is a strange fact: your mother has never once crossed the fields to the canal to seek you out in your hiding place beneath the Drumm Road bridge. Though Momma knows from your brothers where you probably are. For Momma is the gravedigger's wife, grown fearful of leaving the house, made anxious by open fields, the proximity of Drumm Road, where strangers — or neighbors — might drive past and see her.

You have no way of understanding your mother nor even of understanding your ignorance. You have no way of understanding your father's rage except to shrink from it.

Yet now your mother is calling you, and you have no choice but to return home. You are fearful of being punished but you have no choice. What a sight you are — skin itching from a dozen insect bites, snarls in your hair, face sticky and dirty. As soon as you enter the house Momma grabs at you, digging her fingers into your hair.

Rebecca, you bad girl! Where have you been!

Momma is angry, but Momma is relieved, too. She gives you a little shake, then hugs you. So tight, the breath is squeezed out of you. Almost you can believe there are two Mommas, one hard as the ironing board and the other soft as a pillow, one to be feared and the other to be loved. This is the Momma you love saying in a lowered, chiding voice *Go wash, don't let your father see you looking like a little savage.* Pappa is not in the house but working in the cemetery so you are safe with your mother, who strokes your sweaty face with her hands that are dry and wrinkled with an earthen glaze across their backs, a crosshatching of broken capillaries, for Momma's hands, like Pappa's, are a laborer's hands now. *And don't let Pappa know where you've been. I won't be able to spare you if you do.*

Momma kisses your sticky forehead, hugs you another time, and with a sigh gives you a little shove, away.

looked miserably at my mother and leaned back in his chair with a wish in his eyes for the world to just this once stop its relentless spinning and let him get home from work good and have a few minutes to cuss Jesse Helms when he came on WRAL offering his editorial viewpoint (which seemed to be the thing that relaxed my father the way golf or chair bottom recaning or gin soothed other men), then pushed back his own chair and took off after her, in the panel van, up the two miles to town, my brothers reached for more Hamburger Helper and pressure-cooked field peas, bored with the whole scene, but my little sister and I traded looks of silent yet emphatic agreement: Dawg, we got to see this.

Up the two miles to town. When I think of my childhood, I think mostly of those two miles, for childhood is memory, and memory landscape. We bumped along the quarter mile of country road that led to the highway, caught up with my sister at the intersection with old 421. We followed her past the barbed-wire fencing of the prison camp, where a few years later my buddy Sam and I would speak to a prisoner through the fence who would offer us fifty dollars to plant a change of street clothes in the bushes nearby. She sashayed past Sam's daddy's body shop, with its jungle of broken-down vehicles among which, in too few years, Sam and I would sneak our first frosty beers.

My sister's stride was all-get-out uppity. You *knew* not to mess with her, the way those couple miles fell wayside under her what-you-looking-at gait. She churned past the old Mill Outlet, where my little sister and I were often dragged by my mother when she went through her make-your-own-clothes stage, churning out stretch-and-sew T-shirts, excessively neck-holed but vibrantly banded in surfer-cool stripes. The Mill Outlet was nothing more than bolts of fabric lined up in a room smelling of everything fried and Salem Light smoke. Glen Campbell was always on the radio, as if he had his own station. He was a lineman for the county. Something was gentle on that man's mind. Most of the employees and patrons of the Mill Outlet were grossly overweight, but my little sister and I could see only ankles and feet, for we spent the endless time playing beneath the fixtures, making camps among the forest of fabric bolts.

We coasted a few car lengths behind her, under the overpass where Sam and I would bloody our index fingers and carve our initials into a rusty girder one sentimental junior high night. Usually my little sister and I asked my father to sound his horn up under there, for the echo that resulted lingered forlornly as a train whistle, but under the circumstances — my sister exhibiting some stripe of insouciance I'd never seen in anyone before — horn tapping seemed tacky. We passed Kivett's, maker of steeples, and we stared as always at the products listing in the yard, awaiting the deacons of country churches to come by and load them up in their wobbly-wheeled trailers.

Then we were hard on McKoy Street, our town's black main drag. I watched a black boy I knew from school pop out of the screen door of a streetside bungalow, sit down on a green metal glider, take a bite out of something wrapped in a napkin, and stare with only the slightest interest at the white girl marching up the gutter in front of his house, her little white brother in the junk-ass truck behind waving self-consciously. In front of the old black high school, a team of girls stopped their rope jumping to check out my sister's progress. That girl right there is *moving*, I heard one of them say, and then there was laughter, which my sister acknowledged with only an inscrutable glance flung back over her shoulder.

I might well have wondered, *Is my dad following my sister because the only way into town is up McKoy?* But my dad was editor of the newspaper, fiercely opposed to segregation and all brands of bigotry, and I know he would have followed my sister into town that evening if her route had taken her through the country club. My sister paid no attention at all to the shift from country white people's houses to what was now the staunchly black middle-class section of McKoy, the neat brick homes of teachers and ministers and shop owners. Nor did she seem to realize what lay a block or two behind those kempt houses: potholed and muddy lanes fronted by boarded-up shotguns, which I would discover myself a few years later when Sam and I would learn how to buy beer from the boot-legging daddy of a classmate named Big Betty, fifty cents a can.

My sister was gaining on town. There was not a whole lot to gain on — a few blocks of storefronts, fish markets and hot dog joints, barbershops and drugstores — but the alleys behind those storefronts, to those of us reared out among the tobacco fields, accustomed to tractor hum and tree-frog song, were as gray-urban as anything in the big mythic city.

I found myself getting fretful. Something bad seemed about to happen to my sister, and to me, and to my little sister too, though surely I was next in line. I remembered a movie I had watched with my older siblings on a night when my parents were away, one of those fifties horror movies where the camera follows the point of view of the monster, who never appears until the last couple of frames. I wanted my father to slap the gas pedal with his wingtip, quit coasting as if nothing much were at stake, roar up alongside my sister, order her into the back of the van. I wanted to hear those double doors click shut on the paddy wagon, wanted for us to ferry the prisoner back to her cell.

And in ways I want this still, for now I have my own daughter and she's going on fourteen years herself, and I know the day is nigh when she'll take off from the table and I'll no more be able to do much but sigh at the spinning world, rise, and follow lamely along behind.

My sister flew past the Coffeehouse, a game room set up for the youth of the town to have somewhere safe to go, though the black lights and posters were a little too groovy, and the Episcopal minister's wife who routinely volunteered to chaperone strummed Jim Croce songs on her acoustic guitar, driving everyone out on the sidewalk. She passed Leon's Clothiers, Kaleel's Grill. She was gaining on the courthouse, the center of town, but as she started across Main, something shifted. Suddenly, instead of a monster stalking her, a presence she could not shake, the panel van trailing her was more like an escort, a motorcade like the ones I'd seen on television flanking parading dignitaries.

She's up in town now, and she marches like she will march on the night of the next home football game. My sister, see, is a majorette. She twirls fire. They cut the lights in the stadium and crying babies are quieted and the undertow of trash talk dies down slowly. A freshman girl is selected to flick the Zippo. The tiny flame quivers in her nervous hand but my sister, a silhouette, is unflinching. The ends of her arms blaze. She wields fire. My little sister and I push up behind the marching band to see better. We see bugs drawn to the flames our sister twirls, and in that buggy light we notice her shoulders tense slightly as she tosses her lit baton to the heavens and lands perfectly the catch to the oohs and ahs of over half our town.

My father puts his foot on the brake. We're caught at the courthouse stoplight. My little sister and I smile straight ahead at our disappearing sister and the trails of fire lacing the settling-down darkness up in town.

ALEXS PATE

 Innocence Found

One day this past spring, I walked out of my house, on my way to do errands, when I was immediately hit by an overwhelming sense of sadness. It was such a bright wondrous day, and the heavy sweet smell of blooming lilacs swirled around me. It should have made me happy, joyous. But instead it was the certain way the sunlight careened off the buildings and sidewalks or the smell of spring or a combination of both that swept me into the past. And no matter how bucolic or sun-swept my memories of the past may be, they almost always leave me sad. And so this story ends in a sadness of sorts, a caution, so to speak.

I grew up in North Philadelphia, not far from the Philadelphia Zoo and enmeshed in a neighborhood of intensity. It was a neighborhood of working-class black folks who had grabbed on to the promise of the American Dream and were barely holding on. But on my street the sun did shine and Saturdays were full of purposeful activities like cleaning the house and turning the garden hose on cement sidewalks in front of the houses.

As a child, I used to love pickles. Dill, Jewish, sour, sweet-and-sour, hot, or sweet, it didn't matter. Even thinking this now brings a rush of saliva to my mouth. I attended an elementary school a block and a half from my house, and so I'd always run home at lunchtime, eat the food my mother prepared (usually some sort of sandwich and a bowl of soup), and then I'd do or say whatever I had to in order to get out of the house. And with the fifteen or twenty minutes I had left before the afternoon bell rang, I would set out for Little John's.

Little John's was one of those little, idiosyncratic stores one can always find in the inner city. A store that might carry an astonishing variety of goods — from penny candy to staples, from bread to balloons — but does so in the space barely large enough for ten people to stand in without touching. But Little John's was even more unusual in that it was a corner store that was actually located in the middle of the block. For the life of me, I can't quite figure out how John had accomplished such a feat. It was on Seybert Street, a couple of blocks away in the opposite direction from my school. I remember that as you approached the store you'd be gently assaulted by a makeshift wooden enclosed stairway that jutted straight out of the block of row houses. It would almost stop you from walking unimpeded down the street, forcing a kid like me to wonder what lay inside this odd edifice.

You must understand that in Philadelphia's inner city, so many of the houses are exactly the same, conjoined like a series of train cars being pulled toward the Delaware River or somewhere off into the distance, depending almost completely on the creative and financial resources of the residents to distinguish them from one another. It is a good thing that there are addresses. That's all I'm saying.

So Little John's was a small wonder. And inside Little John's there was always a barrel full of pungent brine. And swimming in that brine were the largest dang dill pickles you'd ever seen. Bigger than any pickles I've seen since. And it wasn't just that they were big. They were fully pickled, so thoroughly saturated that the first bite would sometimes might close your mouth altogether in a tight vinegared clinch.

So what I'm saying is that I'd rush from my mother's wholesome Campbell's soup lunch (for which I now realize I owe such an amazing debt) and head straight for Little John's. There, for a mere quarter, I would dive into that barrel and spear my catch.

And from there I was destined back to school, obviously unconcerned with the damage that pickle might do to my natural cologne.

I remember walking out of Little John's with this big pickle and literally skipping up the street. Skipping, I tell you. And in this memory the sun fanned brilliant light all about and the bricks were vivid red and the asphalt the deepest black . . . and I was just so happy. This is proof! I was innocent then. Only someone who is without guilt can skip. The slightest weight of guilt will take the skip out of your gait. But on this day there were no suspicious eyes on me. No sense of outsiderness. Of being the son of a demon. Of being a demon. Nor a criminal. I was just the happiest little colored boy, sucking on my dill pickle and tra-la-laing home. And you have to know there is an art to eating a pickle. But I will refrain from the details of this joy, for in a world colored by a brilliant but only half right pioneer psychotherapist, who shall not be named here, my description would almost certainly be misinterpreted.

It must then suffice to say that I know that once I was innocent. And by innocent I mean that I knew the world was open to me. That I was "without guilt." That no one suspected me of any crime. How special this was for an African American boy. To be able to skip effortlessly down the street. But more to the point, imagine how rare it is today. Black boys are suspected of criminal intent so early in their lives these days they hardly ever get a full measure of innocence. Which, by the way, I believe is essential to be a healthy adult. We *must* know what it means to feel innocent. It is one of the most significant benchmarks in a person's life.

I know that my mother understood this and did the only thing a parent can do: she tried, in so many ways, to preserve my innocence as long as she could. No one else told me that no matter how smart you are and how much you believe that you can do anything you put your mind to, the truth is the energy that you need to be whole in this culture will be taken from you as a rite of passage. Those are your dues as a black person in America. You must give up your innocence, be seen as guilty, eventually feel guilty before you even get a chance to demonstrate your potential.

My mother was tireless when it came to protecting me from the realities of inner-city African American life, but in one way, especially, she was a titan. She watched my teachers like a hawk. She was always in school, at meetings with the principal, the teachers, anybody who'd stop long enough to talk about my performance in school. And, to be sure, in the early days of my education, I have fond memories of my teachers.

And then I found myself in Mr. Baker's class. Mr. Baker was a gaunt white man whose skin seemed to sink into the angled bones of his face. He taught the fifth and sixth grades. I can look back now and realize that he was probably out of his water trying to teach in the inner city. That he probably should have been an insurance or furniture salesman, but there he was standing in front of us. And Mr. Baker had an unpredictable mean streak, and since light corporal punishment was still allowed in the schools, he was a man just this side of being in control.

We accepted his violent outbursts as adult/teacher prerogative. Perhaps my mother overheard some of the kids talking about him, but all of a sudden she started asking me a lot of questions about him. Was he nice? What books were we reading? And so, when I came home one day and told her about a boy that Mr. Baker had slapped, she was genuinely interested.

"You mean he slapped him right in front of the whole class?"

My mother has always been an exuberant woman. She was small, about five feet one, with a creamy, spellbinding smile. There was a bounce in her movement. Excitement just below the sound of her voice. And I knew she loved me. If I have ever known anything, ever been completely sure of anything, it is that my mother loved me absolutely. Even when she got mad at me, it never boiled over. It was always expressed as exasperation, disappointment, or disillusionment.

"No. He never does it that way. If he gets mad at you," I told her, "he makes you go into the cloakroom. He hits you in there." In our school, built at the turn of the century, there were dark, tight little walk-in closets with lines of little hooks on which we were to put our coats. Boots and galoshes lined the floor during bad weather.

"So you didn't see it."

"No, but I heard it." We all had. The boy, Ronald — we called him Peanut, because his closely shaved head was shaped just like the talking peanut on television commercials — had pushed Mr. Baker beyond the limit.

We sat stiff as chocolate saltwater taffy as they disappeared into the coatroom. We sat there quietly waiting. And then, like a muffled gunshot, we heard Mr. Baker's hand smash across Peanut's smooth head. Mr. Baker emerged a second later. It was his practice to make students who had been invited to the coatroom wait until recess or the end of the day before they came out.

Later in the schoolyard, Peanut said that Mr. Baker had come into the dark cloakroom, stared at him for a minute, and without saying a word popped him upside the head.

"He must have done something wrong, Lane, what did he do?" Everybody in my family calls me Lane. Somehow they extracted it from my middle name.

"I don't know, Mom — I think he was talking or something. I don't know what he did." And that was the truth. When punishment was forthcoming in class, the cause had a way of fading into chalk dust.

I don't think my mother believed that Peanut hadn't done *something* to demand such a corporal response. And it wasn't very long before I found myself ordered there as well. I can't remember what I did. It doesn't matter. I'm not sure it mattered then. There is a part of me that feels that Mr. Baker was simply slowly working his way through the class, unconsciously reminding us that we were guilty of something.

There have been many times when I knew what the outcome of a certain event would be, knew ahead of time that it was going to be painful, knew that I was going to get my butt burned, and I always deal with it in the same way. I imagine myself as a blade of grass in a billowing wind. I am surrounded by other blades of grass and we are all moving in the same direction. We have given ourselves up to the wind. We let it take us, because it is fruitless to fight. We swing with the energy of the force facing us instead of working against it. Instead of trying to stand straight up, we bend. Tomorrow is soon enough to stand straight.

I knew he was going to hit me. It was my turn. I gathered my breath and walked ahead of him into the coatroom. The air there was still and funky with the resident odors held by the coats of my inner-city classmates.

It was almost completely dark after he closed the door behind him. His chalk-stained blue serge suit, the one of two that he always wore to class, disappeared. All I saw was his egg-shaped head. His narrow chin nuzzled the darkness. He looked into my eyes. I know he could see that I was terrified, that I was close to tears, but he showed just the slightest of smiles and said, "Turn around."

I did as I was told. And as I faced the other end of the closet, I heard him say, "You will learn." And then I felt his bony hand slam into the back of my head. It knocked me forward at least two steps. I was reeling.

"Do not leave until I tell you." The door opened and closed. I was alone with my stinging head. And my tears. I had to stay in the closet for about two hours, the end of school.

I ran the entire block and a half home. I knew my mother would be home. Even though I'd seen it coming, I couldn't believe that he had actually hit me. That he didn't know my mother, Mrs. Lois Pate, a woman who loved me completely, who was very involved in school activities, who was one of the most respected of all the neighborhood women, and who would not stand for this kind of treatment. Who did he think he was?

"Mom, Mr. Baker hit me. He hit me."

I remember feeling so large, like a balloon swelling in the living room of our North Philadelphia red-brick row house. I filled that entire room. I wasn't hurt now. The look on my mother's face was enough to erase that hurt. To make me feel important. And then I could see her steel herself through the necessary investigation. She asked me what I had done. Why he had gotten so angry. I told her the best I could. But I reminded her that at least ten other people in the class had received the same treatment. We weren't all that bad. And then she was silent.

At dinner she told my father, who fixed his eyes on hers. "He did what?"

"He smacked him."

"For what? Why?" My father was a large-framed, round-headed, caramel-colored man whose gentleness could explode into a raging fury.

"Does it matter, Elec?" My father's name was Alexander, but my mother called him Elec.

"It doesn't matter," she repeated. "There is no reason for that man to put his hands on my child. I'm not having it. I'm going to see the principal tomorrow. I'm telling you, I'm not having some white man hit my child in a classroom."

My father nodded and looked at me. In his look I knew that he approved. He probably was thinking how lucky I was to have such a strong advocate.

My mother went to the school. I remember sitting in Mr. Baker's class, knowing that at any minute he would be summoned to the office just like one of his students and reprimanded. I knew he would get his comeuppance.

I didn't have to wait long. There was a knock on one of the twelve panes of glass in the classroom door. Mr. Baker crossed the floor to open it and was invited outside. This was better than I had hoped for. I turned to the girl sitting next to me, Annette, and smiled. "He's in for it." I said it loud enough for everyone to hear.

And then the principal's head popped in the door. He was bald-headed and round. But he and my mother had developed a good relationship, and he was always nice to me. His eyes instantly found mine. "Alexs, can I see you out here, please?"

I turned and looked around the room. I was a little shaken by this unfolding of events. I thought everything would happen in the office; I didn't think I'd be dragged into it.

I stumbled around two desks as I walked to the door. Mr. Brown, the principal, put his arm around my shoulders and guided me out. "How are you today?" He said softly.

I barely heard him. I nodded my head, but my eyes were on Mr. Baker, who stood directly in front of me. His face was stone, his body completely motionless. There was sweat across his forehead. I had never seen a white man so afraid before. My mother stood just behind Mr. Brown. I guess she wanted enough distance to take this all in.

I imagine that she felt very good at that moment. When you have been victimized all of your life, it is an incredible rush of satisfaction when you can will justice into being.

Mr. Baker thought that I was just another poor black inner-city victim waiting to grow up. Just another African American boy waiting for his number and his cemetery plot or cell. But Mr. Baker did not know Lois Pate. He hadn't been at the school when she forced the principal to personally give me a reading test and then admit that the books that they were giving me to read were at least two grades below my ability. What Mr. Baker did not know was that this episode was only one in a long list of situations in which my mother had gone to whatever lengths she had to to ensure that I held on to a sense of wonder and innocence.

My mother was fighting for my future. She would not let me believe that I was destined to be a negative statistic. She would not let me think that school was a place I couldn't feel completely comfortable in. She would not let me think that she didn't love me or that my life wasn't valuable, that maybe my innocence was less important than Mr. Baker's guilt. She was willing to see him go down to save me. I have never forgotten that.

But as I said, these recollections lead to sadness. I can't help but admit that my mother's attempts to preserve my innocence were woefully inadequate. She could not compete with the force of society throwing labels at me. In the end, the image of Little John's and me skipping along the street is one of the few moments of innocence I can remember. And so I spend my days now, in between my work and the routine matters of life, trying to reacquire much of that lost innocence, which was mine by birth but which I never got to experience.

 Summer Coming

Summer is coming soon. I can feel it in the softening of the air, but I can see it too in the textbooks on my children's desks. The number of uncut pages at the back grows smaller and smaller. The looseleaf is ragged at the edges, the binder plastic ripped at the corner. An old remembered glee rises inside me. Summer is coming. Uniform skirts in mothballs. Pencils with their points left broken. Open windows. Day trips to the beach. Pickup games. Hanging out.

How boring it was.

Of course, it was the making of me, as a human being and a writer. Downtime is where we become ourselves, looking into the middle distance, kicking at the curb, lying on the grass or sitting on the stoop and staring at the tedious blue of the summer sky. I don't believe you can write poetry or compose music or become an actor without downtime, and plenty of it, a hiatus that passes for boredom but is really the quiet moving of the wheels inside that fuel creativity.

And that, to me, is one of the saddest things about the lives of American children today. Soccer leagues, acting classes, tutors — the calendar of the average middle-class kid is so over the top that soon Palm Pilots will be sold in Toys R Us. Our children are as overscheduled as we are, and that is saying something.

This has become so bad that parents have arranged to schedule times for unscheduled time. Earlier this year the privileged suburb of Ridgewood, New Jersey, announced a Family Night, when there would be no homework, no athletic practices, and no after-school events. This was terribly exciting until I realized that this was not one night a week, but one single night. There is even a free time movement, and Web site: Family Life 1st. Among the frequently asked questions provided online: "What would families do with family time if they took it back?"

Let me make a suggestion for the kids involved: how about nothing? It is not simply that it is pathetic to consider the lives of children who don't have a moment between piano and dance and homework to talk about their day or just search for split ends, an enormously satisfying leisure-time activity of my youth. There is also ample psychological research suggesting that what we might call "doing nothing" is when human beings actually do their best thinking, and when creativity comes to call. Perhaps we are creating an entire generation of people whose ability to think outside the box, as the current parlance of business has it, is being systematically stunted by scheduling.

A study by the University of Michigan quantified the down-time deficit; in the last twenty years American kids have lost about four unstructured hours a week. There has even arisen a global Right to Play movement: in the Third World it is often about child labor, but in the United States it is about the sheer labor of being a perpetually busy child. In Omaha a group of parents recently lobbied for additional recess. Hooray, and yikes.

How did this happen? Adults did it. There is a culture of adult distrust which suggests that a kid who is not playing softball or attending science enrichment programs — or both — is huffing or boosting cars: if kids are left alone, they will not stare into the middle distance and consider the meaning of life and how come your nose in pictures never looks the way you think it should, but instead will get into trouble. There is also the culture of cutthroat and unquestioning competition that leads even the parents of pre-schoolers to gab about prestigious colleges without a trace of irony: this suggests that any class in which you do not enroll your first-grader will put him at a disadvantage in, say, law school.

Finally, there is a culture of workplace presence (as opposed to productivity). Try as we might to suggest that all these enrichment activities are for the good of the kid, there is ample evidence that they are really for the convenience of parents with way too little leisure time of their own. Stories about the resignation of presidential aide Karen Hughes unfailingly reported her dedication to family time by noting that she arranged to get home at 5:30 one night a week to have dinner with her son. If one weekday dinner out of five is considered laudable, what does that say about what's become normative?

Summer is coming. It used to be a time apart for kids, a respite from the clock and the copybook, the organized day. Every once in a while, either guilty or overwhelmed or tired of listening to me keen about my monumental boredom, my mother would send me to some rinky-dink park program that consisted almost entirely of three-legged races and making things out of Popsicle sticks. Now there are music camps, sports camps, fat camps, probably thin camps instead. I mourn hanging out in the back yard. I mourn playing wiffle ball in the street without a sponsor and matching shirts. I mourn drawing in the dirt with a stick.

Maybe that kind of summer is gone for good. Maybe this is the leading edge of a new way of living that not only has no room for contemplation but is contemptuous of it. But if downtime cannot be squeezed during the school year into the life of frantic and often joyless activity with which our children are saddled while their parents pursue frantic and often joyless activity of their own, what about summer? Do most adults really want to stand in line for Space Mountain or sit in traffic to get to a shore house that doesn't have enough saucepans? Might it be even more enriching for their children to stay at home and do nothing? For those who say they will only watch TV or play on the computer, a piece of technical advice: the cable box can be unhooked, the modem removed. Per-

haps it is not too late for American kids to be given the gift of en-
forced boredom for at least a week or two, staring into space,
bored out of their gourds, exploring the inside of their own heads.
"To contemplate is to toil, to think is to do," said Victor Hugo.
"Go outside and play," said Prudence Quindlen. Both of them
were right.

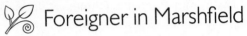 Foreigner in Marshfield

I moved to the United States from Japan when I was five years old, after my parents divorced. My arrival in my father's hometown of Marshfield, Wisconsin, was announced in the daily paper — Jack Revoyr, the prodigal son of Ronald and Mildred, had returned with a half-breed child. Most people in Marshfield already knew I existed — twice, when they were married, my father brought my mother home to visit, and for many of my grandparents' neighbors and friends, she was the first Asian that they'd ever laid eyes on. I'd come along on one of those two-week trips, when I was a baby, but in 1974 I was brought there to live. My father left me with my grandparents while he went to work in New York, making me the newest, most reluctant citizen of Marshfield. To my knowledge, I was the only person of color in the entire town of fourteen thousand people. Almost all the things I know about the workings of race I learned in the time that I spent there.

I lived in my grandparents' house for a little over two years. And I did live, mostly, *in* the house, looking out at the neighborhood from my father's old room, making up stories to pass the time. Marshfield scared me — a small, isolated town in the middle of Wisconsin, it seemed untouched by the social upheavals, the movements and debates around racial and sexual equality, that opened up the collective mind of the rest of the country in the 1960s and 1970s. The town itself was unspectacular, but it was surrounded by beautiful farmland and forest, which was dotted here and there with clean, clear lakes and small, slow-moving streams. The smells of beer and bratwurst seemed to linger in the air, always, mixing with the scent of fresh-cut grass. Most of the people who lived in Marshfield worked there too, for the meat-processing plant, or the cheese manufacturers, or the factories that made hunting clothes and shoes. For those who were born there, the town was both trap and protection. Almost all of my father's classmates got factory jobs right out of high school — or sometimes before — married, and had families by the time they were twenty. For a few, like my father, Marshfield was a place that needed to be escaped from, although he was warned by his teachers not to leave and go to college, because the outside world was sinful and corrupting. And for outsiders, like me, people who tried to make some kind of home there, Marshfield was excluding, impenetrable.

Moving to a small, white, midwestern town from the huge, bustling, international city of Tokyo was a tremendous shock to my system, and while my English was fluent — I'd gone to an American school in Tokyo — it still didn't come as naturally as Japanese. Marshfield, for its part, was no more ready for me, and the townspeople made it clear I wasn't welcome. They hadn't approved of my father's departure, and they'd been scandalized by his marriage; now, in their eyes, he was flaunting evidence of his bad behavior; he was inflicting on them the terrible fruit of his sins. But because they couldn't punish him directly, they focused their disapproval on his child. Both adults and children glared and sometimes swore at me if I passed them on the sidewalk. No one would sit next to us when my grandparents took me to church. Young boys used me for target practice when I rode around town on my bike, and I discovered that apples, if thrown accurately and hard, can hurt just as much as rocks. When the occasional child — out of sympathy or boredom or plain curiosity — made some preliminary gesture of friendship, her parents would soon put a stop to it. Because of the war, the children would tell me, and I didn't understand until much later what they meant. Many of the town's fathers and grandfathers had served in World War II, and to them I wasn't just a foreigner: I was the Enemy.

When school started, things only got worse. I couldn't hide in my grandparents' house anymore, and school was a string of disasters. I got beaten up in the bathroom so many times that I developed a huge and resilient bladder, which could go an entire school day without needing to be relieved. Strange kids would call me "Jap" or "Nip" or "Yellow-bellied murderer." Groups of older students would corner me in the hallway, force me to count to ten in Japanese, and then mockingly try to imitate my words. Sometimes teachers, walking by, would put a stop to this. More often they just kept walking.

Simply getting back and forth from the elementary school — which was about a mile away — was like picking my way through a minefield. Certain kids would chase me or try to make me late, and while there were several of them, both boys and girls, one girl remains distinct in my memory. Her name was Jean — I don't recall her last name — and she lived at the vertex of a V in the road about halfway to the school. Both sides of the V eventually crossed the street where the old brick building stood, flanking the school on either side with straight, separating arms, so it didn't matter which way I took. But every morning as I approached, I'd see Jean waiting. She was a couple of years older than me, and about twice as big, with dark, curly hair and an olive complexion. When she saw me coming, she'd brighten up and yell out some curse or warning. She'd tell me I wasn't going to make it past her that day, or she'd announce that I had to get off her road. Often she'd ask the question posed by kids all over town. "Hey, weirdo," she'd say. "What *are* you?" I wouldn't answer — perhaps because I was trying to figure that out myself — and besides, in that moment, simple survival was more important than reflection. I'd make some fancy foot move, fake and jab, and then cut to one side of the V. After a few forays in each direction, I realized that I naturally seemed to go left — a characteristic that followed me all the way through my college basketball days. The road to the left was slightly longer, with cracked, uneven sidewalks, a dramatic jut uphill. But it was the road I preferred. Sometimes Jean managed to head me off completely, and I had to take a more roundabout way to school. But sometimes, despite the fact that she overplayed that side, I got past her and ran down the left side of the V, Jean yelling that she'd get me tomorrow.

While the rest of the kids in Marshfield acted like hassling me was a game, Jean's treatment was different, more personal. My grandparents told me she was Jewish, and it took me years to appreciate the significance of this detail — she too was unaccepted in the entirely Christian town, but with my arrival, she moved up one notch on the town's totem pole, and she wanted to make sure I knew where I belonged.

Things got easier in Marshfield my second year, which was when my grandfather taught me to fight. Ronnie Revoyr — known as Frenchie because of his French Canadian parents — was a first-rate hunter and marksman who'd worked his whole life in a shoe factory and then a chicken-slaughtering plant. He was a bigoted man — he used racial epithets freely, and had refused to attend my parents' wedding — but it enraged him that the town did not embrace me. When a group of teenagers chased me home, my grandfather went out to the yard in his work pants and undershirt and challenged them all to a fight. When my grandmother's cousin told me I was going to hell because of my dirty yellow blood, my grandfather threw her out of the house. I've always wondered what it was like for him to see his only grandchild subjected to the racism that he himself perpetuated. Because my grandfather, for all of his faults, loved me. One day, while he was spraying Bactine on my knees after someone had knocked me off my bike, he bit his lip and his eyes filled with tears. He told me then, voice shaking with anger, not to run away anymore — to stand up to the kids who were mean to me and fight. He taught me how to punch, how to defend myself against incoming blows, how to throw rocks back with accuracy and strength. They were lessons I made use of in the following year, and the irony strikes me only now: it was my grandfather, the uneducated, racist, small-town white man, who taught me how to survive as a person of color.

Just before I left Marshfield forever, something incredible happened — a young black couple, the Millers, moved into town, drawn by work at the growing regional clinic. They moved, in fact, right onto my grandparents' block, just a few houses up and across the street. The intense, swirling hatred that had surrounded me for two years was transferred at once to the Millers. This change was not remarkable to me, even when I was seven; I knew what the people of Marshfield thought of blacks. What *was* remarkable was that suddenly *I* was included in the discussion. The same kids who'd informed me that I was "the Enemy" now spoke of the dangers embodied by the Millers. The same parents who had crossed the street to get away from me now instructed *me* to cross the street to avoid the Millers. But my memories of my own experiences were far too fresh; unlike Jean, I couldn't replicate, onto someone else, the things I had endured. So I took what, for me, seemed like radical measures — I smiled at the Millers whenever I saw them, said hello when they passed me on the sidewalk. I learned, at seven, a lesson I've known ever since — that I had more in common with the Millers than with the people who were suddenly trying to include me, the people who'd tormented us both.

I carry scars from my two years in Marshfield, and the absence of things that are irretrievably lost. My first language was Japanese, but through willful denial and disuse, I'd mostly forgotten it by the time I left Marshfield. Close to each of my parents in Japan, I felt disconnected from them both in America — my father because he was white, and my mother because she never experienced racism until she moved to the United States as an adult, and because when people *did* refer to her as Jap, or Chink, or Gook, she had the strength to tell them — as *I* couldn't as a child — to at least get the country right and to go to hell.

But there were positive elements to my experience in Marshfield, too. The hours I spent locked inside, reading or making up stories or listening to my grandfather's tales, were training time, apprenticeship, for my eventually becoming a writer. And the town made clear, in no uncertain terms, the workings and significance of race. It let me know exactly where I stood, and when my father moved us, thankfully, out of Wisconsin, there was never any question — as there might have been if I'd lived in a more accepting environment — that I was a child of color. I learned to take pride in what made me different, to define that difference rather than letting someone else define it for me. And so Los Angeles, when I moved here, was nothing less than heaven — I heard Japanese again, and ate Japanese food for the first time since I'd come to America. But it wasn't just being around Japanese Americans that pleased me. Los Angeles is a smorgasbord of color and culture — and if L.A. is a city of racial division and strict boundaries, it's also a place where those boundaries are constantly being blurred, where accepted terms are redefined daily. In my high school in Culver City, over forty different languages were spoken. Asian kids listened to hip-hop and jazz. African American kids were fluent in Spanish. I took my black and Chicano basketball teammates to Japanese dances in the Japanese American town of Gardena. In L.A. I also met a number of mixed-race children, and it was the first place where I experienced the simple comfort of finding others who looked like me. Here, people still made racial assumptions about me, but they were somehow less insidious, sometimes charming. An old woman on my block regularly addressed me in Spanish, refusing to believe I didn't have Mexican blood. Someone would ask me at least once a week if I was Native American. Occasionally, when I had a tan in the summer, and especially when I went through my regrettable pseudo–Jheri Curl stage, people even thought I was a light-skinned black girl. And there were also those who assumed I was white, and who couldn't understand why I didn't take that as a compliment. But here, in Los Angeles, it was clear I belonged, even if no one knew quite where to place me. In L.A. I never felt like what I always was in Marshfield — the only Asian kid, the enemy, the freak.

I would never want to relive the years I spent in central Wisconsin, or wish them on anyone else. But I'm grateful for the time I spent there. One's piecing together of one's own identity is a lifetime proposition in any case, but for me the project was both complicated and simplified by the two years I lived with my grandparents. When I came to this country, with my white father, and into a white community, my identity could have developed in one of many directions. But because of those punishing experiences in Marshfield, I learned firsthand that this country's thoughts and fears about immigration are inextricably linked to race; I know that there are clear demarcations between whites and everyone else; and I know which side of the fence I belong on. I remember Jean, who waited for me at the vertex of the V, making me choose to go one direction or the other. I chose the side that was more difficult, but it was the one I leaned toward naturally. And I've also come to realize that there really *was* no choice — no matter which way I decided to go, the two roads ended at the same destination.

FAITH RINGGOLD

 The Boy Nobody Knew

It was one of those hot summer nights in Harlem in 1937. Mother, Daddy, and Uncle Hilliard were talking about their childhood growing up in Jacksonville, Florida. When Uncle Hilliard came to visit we never missed a chance to laugh at his stories. Everything he said was funny. We kids would just cover our mouths and laugh into our hands. As long as we were quiet, Mother would forget it was late and we were still up.

Uncle Hilliard was at the door now saying goodbye. Each of us kids could give him a hug and he'd give us a silver dollar to spend on our vacation.

Soon school would be closed and in a few weeks we'd be going to stay with the Pattersons and their kids in Atlantic City. Barbara and Andrew would spend their silver dollars long before then, but I saved mine in my piggy bank. When Mother needed some cash she'd borrow from me, replacing the coins with buttons and washers, though it would be years before I found that out.

"You sure are crazy, Hilliard," Mother yelled down the stairs at Uncle Hilliard; he'd told my father, "Now don't you get no uglier till I get back. You need a license now to walk the street." Daddy just laughed and laughed.

And then the house was quiet. We were getting ready for bed when we heard the superintendent running up the stairs and knocking on every door. "Fire! Fire! Everybody outside!"

Everyone's doors opened and all the tenants poured into the

halls of our tiny five-story apartment building and down the narrow, steep stairs into the street.

It was really late by then, and the streets were empty except for all of us standing there. Some people were wrapped in sheets over their nightclothes. "Thank goodness it's summer," Mother said. Hardly anybody was fully dressed.

Soon the fire engines woke up the entire street and people came from everywhere to see where the fire was coming from. But it was only in the basement.

The firemen came with their boots and helmets and big fire hoses, and in no time they put out the fire. Afterward they let my brother Andrew and some of the other boys climb up in the fire truck and try on their firemen's hats.

The adults gathered in groups and talked softly so that we kids could hardly hear. There was a new little boy among us whom nobody knew. He was Mr. and Mrs. Mullen's little boy, from the fifth floor.

The superintendent brought him down in a wheelchair. Nobody knew him. Nobody knew he lived there. His mother and father were very quiet people; hardly anyone ever saw them. Mr. Mullen was a night watchman in a warehouse, so he went to work late and came home early. And Mrs. Mullen only came out to buy groceries and go to church on Sunday.

The little boy looked very strange as he sat twisting and turning in his wheelchair and reaching out to the other children, trying to grab their outstretched hands. He attempted to speak, but only grunts came from his mouth.

Some of the tenants remembered hearing strange sounds coming from the Mullens' apartment, and after that they'd hear "Shh, shh." Mrs. Potter, their next-door neighbor, said, "I would have never guessed that they had a little boy living there. We all thought that Mr. and Mrs. Mullen lived alone."

"What's wrong with him?" one of the neighbors asked his mother. "Is he your boy? Does he live in the building?" another neighbor asked. But Mrs. Mullen didn't answer. She just kept looking at her son and he at her. He seemed so happy and she so sad. There were tears in her eyes and his too.

The men in the building gathered around the boy's wheelchair and lifted him up and carried him upstairs. My mother and some of the other mothers put their arms around Mrs. Mullen. "God don't put no more on us than we can bear, Mrs. Mullen," my mother said softly. "We understand."

The next day on our way to school we saw that same boy sitting in his wheelchair across the street in the sun. It was Kenneth Mullen, Jr. We knew now that he was six years old and he had never been out in the sun until now.

They said he had a disease that made him act funny and talk funny, in grunts and groans. But Mr. Parker, who had a medical degree though he worked in the post office, said he was a smart boy in the mind but his body was sick, and that his disease was called multiple sclerosis and there was no known cure for it.

After the fire Mr. and Mrs. Mullen didn't have to hide their little boy anymore. People in the neighborhood now knew him and loved him too.

Everybody going to work and to school stopped by to see him. Just like that, Kenneth Mullen, Jr., was no longer the boy whom nobody knew.

NTOZAKE SHANGE

 Growing Up in St. Louis

Above all else St. Louis was a colored town: "a whiskey black space." That's not to say there were no white people. It's just to say I had to go out of my neighborhood to find some and then they'd wish I hadn't. This may be all new for those born after 1964, but I grew up in St. Louis in the midst of a struggle for the soul of the country, and I'm not talking about *Sputnik*. There was nothing but struggle surrounding us as colored children in America from 1954 on. But aside from some political meetings held in my parents' house late into the night, I just knew there were a lot of Negroes in St. Louis, that I lived among them, and that I was one of them. Race defined my reality, and if more people would admit this it'd be a safer world we live in today. The emblems of my childhood: Emmett Till, bus rides in Montgomery, bombs in Birmingham, and the fires in Watts.

For years my sisters, my brother, and I went to Clark School, which was, luckily, at the end of our block so we had to cross only one boulevard to get there. I had a wonderful teacher, Mrs. Smith, who always looked swank and rouged her cheeks just a wee bit too much. From Mrs. Smith, I learned about decorum and that colored children must always exercise it. Mrs. Smith loved Paul Laurence Dunbar, so anytime she could, his work was what we would read aloud. Now, the problem presented by Dunbar is that it's written in Black English, which we were not encouraged to speak at all. Yet there was Mrs. Smith, letting the '*des* and '*dahs* roll off her tongue with a smile. This was also true of my mother, who lolled in her Dunbar as if she could see Malindy right in front of us, or Ike just as Dunbar described him. So I grew up in this strange world of contradictions.

Yes, we were Americans and my uncles fought in the wars, but we couldn't try on hats in the department store, couldn't eat at most restaurants nor stay at the finest hotels. We could take pride in Hughes and Dunbar, but we mustn't use double negatives if any white people were around. Yes, we ate chitlins, but we mustn't tell anyone. Yes, we traipsed off to the Veiled Prophet Parade like the rest of St. Louis, not realizing we were watching a ritual that grew from white supremacy. The Veiled Prophet himself was cloaked in satin and beaded robes. I think he should have been carrying a burning cross, but then I was drawn into the beauty of it all with the rest of St. Louis. There's something about childhood that finds joy and excitement almost everywhere. All these tidbits about growing up in St. Louis will mean nothing to you if you don't talk about the veneer of elegance that is the city. No matter what kind of house or what neighborhood, there were medians of granite and sculpture at the end of the blocks. The bricks of the houses hid the crumblin' insides of many of them or exalted the many mansions. And oh, the churches and synagogues were just like in the Bible. And our songs, especially: "In my Father's house there are many mansions," which meant to me that there was a colored one for sure.

I stayed at Clark School for two years, surrounded by, as folks like to say, "my own kind" and as happy as I could be. Then one day a woman came to school to see a few of us. She took us in a little room where we had to recite our numbers backward, define words, look at strange images and tell her what they were. It was all very odd. I think maybe ten of us went into this room and were asked to complete logical sequences of objects, ideas, and things. This was the first clue that I was being singled out to join the struggle of my people. But you couldn't have told me this then. The lady came back for a meeting with our parents and told them we had high IQs and belonged in the gifted program, which for us was at Dewey School, far off in a working-class neighborhood.

They didn't tell us that we'd end up being the only colored children around, that we'd have to take a trolley and two buses, or that we weren't welcome where we were going.

Going to Dewey School was nothing like what the children in Little Rock endured. There were no crowds or police, but there was a silence my sister and I met that was hurtful and intimidating. My fifth-grade teacher, Ms. Baldwin, tried to ameliorate the situation. My classmates insisted that I was Greek or Sicilian. It was inconceivable to them that I was a Negro among them. This meant a lot of tightrope walking. I didn't want to do or say anything that might get me beat up. I still wanted to say, "Yes, I am a Negro."

When a brown-skinned boy arrived the next year, my fate was sealed. Robert Alexander and I were paired off together to do projects, to square-dance, you name it. If we had to have partners, Robert had to be mine. It was as if we were being treated "separate but equal" in the very place integration was to happen. But we weathered the togetherness as best we could, exchanging as few words as possible. Here is my contradiction. I'd get on my bus to go home with such relief. Home was nothing but colored people, and every day I couldn't get there soon enough. Yet poor Robert and I couldn't make a go of it in the very white environment we shared every day.

On Windermere Place, where we lived, there were Haitians, Puerto Ricans, regular white people, and us. Something was always going on — double dutch, kickball, Monopoly, or bid whist. We had free rein in the street, since only those who lived on it had the right to drive on it. So we rode our bikes right down the middle of it, or if we felt brave we'd ride up to the parking lot of Harris Teachers College and ride in circles, this when our parents sent out messages that we were "missing" and we got in trouble. But this was not my only world. I lived in the world of books as well.

We were lucky that the Cabanne Street Library was within walking distance, because I walked to it as often as I could — to learn, to feel, in some cases to see. That's where I discovered Susan B. Anthony and Toussaint L'Ouverture. I also read every Nancy Drew there was at the time. I found Carter G. Woodson's "On Facts About the Negro" and Du Bois, Countée Cullen, James Weldon Johnson, Jane Austen and Charlotte Brontë, Wild Bill Hickok, and so many more. My father brought home a mass of socialist literature like *The Ukraine*, with a cover of a white woman surrounded by brilliant roses lauding the success of collective farming. Or he'd have the latest *Science Digest*. Or my mother would sneak books like Baldwin's *Giovanni's Room* or *Mandingo* into the house, but her favorites were Frank Yerby's romance novels, like *Foxes and Harrow*. She took special delight in Yerby because he'd made it in publishing and in Hollywood, never denying he was Negro.

I loved books. I slept with them and tried to eat with them at my side. But Mother insisted that I take part in dinner table discussions, which were really interesting. My parents would facilitate discussions about race and our individual lives. But nothing was like finding a quiet place to hunker down with a stack of books, be they poetry or medical journals. Inside the pages of a book I was totally free. I actually wrote a letter to one journal asking for more information about the newest discovery that could prevent pregnancy. I guess they were taken aback by an eleven-year-old wanting this information, because they wrote me the sweetest reply, explaining that I should speak with my parents about this subject. That makes me laugh now, but then I was very serious. I also wrote away to a physicist who was working on the quantum theory. He wrote me back too. And I felt certain they wouldn't have responded if they'd known I was colored. This is how racism warps one's perceptions. I was raised when these perceptions — ours of white people, and theirs of us — were in violent upheaval and childhood did not last long. Childhood, however, can last forever in many lands and times and adventures and conversations inside the pages of a book. I travel the world from my back porch.

SUSAN RICHARDS SHREVE
 Three Women and Me

This is a small story of three women and me, which took place in a matter of minutes in an amphitheater at Doctor's Hospital in downtown Washington, D.C., in the spring of 1945, when I was five. In attendance were my mother and my pediatrician, Dr. Margaret Mary Nicholson, and the visiting medical miracle worker from Australia, Sister Elizabeth Kenny, and I, who was to be the real star of the show that morning.

Washington was a sultry, damp, disease-ridden swamp city at the end of the Second World War. There was poverty and over-population and illness; the city and its suburbs had been teeming with soldiers stuffed into apartments and rooming houses and other people's houses, like our little one in Silver Spring. Rats and rabid dogs ran in the streets, and hospitals were overcrowded. There was a shortage of doctors and nurses, and in the absence of penicillin, which had been distributed to soldiers overseas, there were epidemics: scarlet fever, spinal meningitis, polio. Polio was the plague for the parents of that generation, lurking in the shadows, then sweeping in with symptoms of influenza that could in a matter of hours paralyze a child, leaving its evidence for the rest of the child's life. In 1945, Sister Kenny, who had developed the first treatment for paralytic polio, based on the application of heat rather than splints, was a box-office hit in the United States, lecturing on her treatment and spreading the word for recovery.

I don't remember Washington at this time, except in frames of flashing pictures. It's difficult now to separate what I might remember from what I've been told or read about in books. But I do remember Sister Kenny.

When I was one year old and living in Toledo, Ohio, I had polio, which was diagnosed by my pediatrician as paralytic strep throat. My mother had never heard of this particular illness — perhaps it existed, perhaps not — but she was told that the paralysis would be gone as soon as the strep bacteria disappeared. By the time my parents discovered that I had had polio, not strep, the virus was gone and the residual damage remained — as it does with polio. And so my mother set about the business of making things right.

Muscles are indiscriminately destroyed by the polio virus, which hits like a random bullet, leaving only traces of muscles. It was my mother's plan to go after the traces. She was a perfectionist, not easily discouraged or bored and with an imagination that filled a room, at least my room. She brought a kind of whimsy and delight to the military regimen of exercises she designed to coax these traces of muscle back to life. To my mind, we played all the time — one game after the other. I didn't even know that I couldn't walk at all, and eventually a day came when I could. I had a sort of jumping-jack gait, but by the time I was three, I could walk.

The year we moved to Washington, the war was ending and everyone was sick. Signs warning of scarlet fever were plastered on the houses where we lived in Silver Spring. There was meningitis. I got rheumatic fever. Or maybe I didn't. I was treated for it, in any case, by Dr. Nicholson, who was the only pediatrician willing to do house calls at night during the war. She came from downtown by bicycle, in a white dress, with hair pinned to the top of her head in a loopy bun that sometimes gave way and fell to her waist, a stethoscope around her neck, a crucifix in her pocket. The treatment was ten Hail Marys, kale sandwiches on brown bread, and cod liver oil. She came every day until I got well. Which never struck me as unusual. She was my doctor, and I was sick.

Just this year I learned that Dr. Nicholson was famous for taking care of the city's poor, which we were not. At a time when blacks couldn't go to the hospitals in segregated Washington, she'd pick up the sickest babies in her bicycle basket, haul them to the hospital, treat them herself in the emergency room, and take them home. She ran her office as a clinic, with mothers and children lining the halls, sitting on the floor, waiting sometimes hours and hours. I know: I was among them, unwilling to leave Dr. Nicholson until I was twenty-one and getting married. She saw each patient, staying into the night, charging what a family could pay or nothing. And she always had a plan for something — orphans in Mexico, leukemia patients in the Deep South, burn victims. She liked my mother, and somehow — I never asked and don't know how it happened — my mother and Dr. Nicholson were in cahoots. Whatever wild scheme the doctor had in mind, my mother was a part of its execution.

Dr. Nicholson's plan for me was that I be the subject of a lecture by the world-famous Sister Kenny in the amphitheater of Doctor's Hospital, in front of hundreds of physicians and residents and interns and nurses.

That morning at breakfast, my mother showed me the picture of Sister Kenny that was on the front page of the newspaper. She looked large and old and had a face which in my memory is that of an executioner. My mother explained to me what would happen at the hospital amphitheater; her voice was contagious with excitement for what I imagined then was my leading role. Only lately have I understood what it was she and Dr. Nicholson hoped would happen that morning.

My mother had spent the last four years inventing her own regimen of exercises for me: hours of standing pencil-straight against the wall, walking with a book on top of my head, sitting on the end of a chair and exercising each tiny muscle in the toes and feet and ankles, the neck and hands and arms, doing stretches, pressing my foot against her hand, my leg against her arm. She had taught me to walk.

My mother was a shy woman, mysterious even to her children. Perhaps she was susceptible to Dr. Nicholson's insistence that Sister Kenny would *want* to know her method, would admire the success she'd had with me in spite of the fact that my mother's method did not include warm cloths, was in fact a contradiction of Sister Kenny's method. My guess in hindsight is that Dr. Nicholson, altruistic as she might have been, had a competitive edge and didn't mind challenging this Australian saint in a public forum.

That morning, riding in the back of a taxicab downtown to Doctor's Hospital, my mother and I were gleeful stage-struck innocents, holding hands in the back seat, swinging around the curves of Rock Creek Parkway, on our way to victory.

Dr. Nicholson met us in front of the hospital with her bicycle, slipped a lollipop into my jacket pocket, had me say ten Hail Marys and the Our Father, made me stick out my tongue so she could see if it was coated, hold out my fingers so she could see if the nails had white spots, and asked me how much I had in my piggy bank for the poor children in Guatemala. Even now I check my tongue in the mirror and look for spots on my nails.

We followed Dr. Nicholson into a room where another child with polio was lying on a stretcher, covered with a sheet. She looked at me, unsmiling.

A nurse came in with another stretcher. My mother lifted me up, took off my clothes — I was wearing a red checked dress with a large collar that I thought looked like a diaper around my neck, and a short leg brace and white tights. A nurse put a hospital gown on me and covered me with a sheet. In the distance, I heard someone talking, a woman with a large voice.

"You'll be wheeled into the theater by a nurse," Dr. Nicholson said. "Your mother and I will be in the front-row seats — if you turn your head, you'll be able to see us. Sister Kenny will stand beside your stretcher and she'll look at your leg and your neck and the right side of your body, and you will lie still and let her look."

"Will she smile?" I asked. My mother told me later that I asked that as if I already had a sense of Sister Kenny.

"Smiling is not her job," Dr. Nicholson said. There was no gentle hand on the arm, no soft words, no kisses with Dr. Nicholson, just her steady presence and high expectations.

That morning my mother was wearing a broad-brimmed black cloth hat with a thin striped silk ribbon around the crown. When I looked over to see if she was in the amphitheater as the nurse pushed my stretcher onto the stage under the bright lights, I saw her in the first row, sitting next to Dr. Nicholson. She looked very beautiful. She always did.

I didn't see Sister Kenny until I was directly beside her. She was looking at the audience, not at me, and from the stretcher, with my angle of perspective slightly skewed, what I saw was an enormous woman who looked like a large man with a square box of a jaw and a booming voice and hands the size of a trucker's. Looking now at a photograph of Sister Kenny I have downloaded from the Internet, I see that she has wide-set eyes and a pretty mouth, an undistinguished jaw, a pleasant expression. She was probably eighteen in the photograph, and that morning she was sixty-five. A lot can happen in a life to change an expression.

"Hello," I said to her. "My name is Susan Richards." My mother had taught me early to go forward, to be the first to speak. "People are sometimes afraid to speak first," she'd say to me, compensating for her own reserve. "So you be the one to help them out." The operative words for me as a little girl were "help them out."

But Sister Kenny wasn't interested in my help.

She looked down, not at my face, and lifted the sheet, or rather tore it off my body in its oversized dressing gown in a grand gesture.

"This is patient Susan Richards, age five, infantile paralysis, November 1941, paralytic polio right side of the body, atrophy of the leg."

The sheet must have dropped to the ground. She leaned over me, not once looking at my face so I'd have a chance for eye contact, a chance to make a friend of this cross-country moving van.

She looked at my legs, my hips, checked my arms, wiggled my ankles and toes, all the time shaking her head, with an expression of desolation on her face.

"The patient has been treated by methods devised by her mother. It is my understanding that these have never included the application of hot cloths or muscle stretching. And so . . ." She lifted me off the stretcher in a swoop, set me on the ground, where I wavered unsteadily, and said, "WALK."

I did walk. I didn't fall, and it seemed to me I walked in a straight enough line, though I limped, of course, because I wasn't wearing braces. I must not have taken more than five or six steps before she lifted me back onto the stretcher and raised her hands in a gesture of defeat.

"By the time she is twelve years old, this child will not be able to walk any longer."

There was, as I remember, a terrible commotion, and out of nowhere Dr. Nicholson gathered me in her arms, flew across the stage, took off my hospital gown, dressed me in my tights and dress, buttoned up my overcoat, tied my hat on, and delivered me to my mother. She didn't say a single word until the end.

"Ten Hail Marys, Susan. Quickly."

I did, and in seconds we were rushing down the corridor of the hospital, my hand in my mother's, out the front door, hailing a cab, and seated side by side in the back, looping through Rock Creek Park.

I was afraid that I'd let my mother down.

She took off her broad-brimmed hat, put it in her lap, and gripped my hand tightly as we swang through the park. Finally she turned to me, saying in her quiet voice, "I am so sorry."

"How come?" I asked, surprised that she thought she should be sorry.

"For what Sister Kenny said to you."

"I didn't believe her," I said, and in the dark safety of the back seat of the taxi, under a canopy of budding trees, I leaned hard against her. "Because you told me I could walk, and I can."

SUSAN STRAIGHT
 Crick

It wasn't really an arroyo, always a romantic word to me; an arroyo is a canyon where water has trickled away the earth, where trees have taken root, a place with a name.

Our magical stream was really a drainage ditch, a flood control channel, carved starkly into the fields between a shopping center and the railroad tracks that bordered our elementary school in Riverside, California.

But there was water. And as children, my brothers and sister and I were always looking for water.

We lived on the edge of the desert, in a land between: between mountain ranges and the ocean, between Los Angeles and Palm Springs. It was hot much of the time, dry, and agricultural when I was growing up. We didn't know many people with pools, and anyway, chlorinated water wasn't what I wanted.

I wanted a stream, like Anne of Green Gables with her babbling brook, which laughed and chattered through a woods. Huck Finn and Tom Sawyer had a huge river, with muddy banks on which to wave at boats and lean fishing poles. Stuart Little's family had the pond in Central Park, where they could race boats.

I wanted a crick, as my father used to call the Colorado streams he fished in when he was a boy. "That's what we called it," he'd say. "We spent hours there." I imagined my own crick, where I could skip round stones found on the banks, where trout circled in pools near the boulders, and where I could cool my feet.

The Santa Ana River was too far to walk, and so on long afternoons when school had ended, or in summer when the heat rippled like false water on our asphalt street, we searched for our own creeks and rivers.

We found the irrigation canals that wound through the orange groves near our house. The water glided in its cement bed, smooth and cool and green, with waving grasses on the bottom and maybe even fish, we thought, staring at flashes of silver that could have been fingerlings or could have been beer tabs twisting in the current. We weren't supposed to swim in the canals, because we'd heard that kids had drowned when caught in one of the grates under the bridge where we dangled our feet now.

But lots of kids did. Their bodies, brown and pale legs and arms, became the fish while I watched. They drifted down the swift silent current, caught the iron ladders, and then leaped in again.

I was too afraid of the slick sides, the dark maw under the wooden bridge.

My brothers and sister and I would head into the groves, where, if the farmer was irrigating, water gurgled inside squat cement pumps at the canal's edge. Then it leapt as if magical, white bubbly ribbons of water arcing out from the small round concrete headers at the end of the rows and down the furrows between the trees.

We squatted at the edges of these small manmade creeks, smelling the water as it met the hot dirt, racing sticks and leaves down the perfectly straight tributaries. But then the water would cease, the streams soak quickly into the thirsty ground under the dusty leaves, and we would move on.

When I was a child, it rained more. I tell my own kids this, and they nod their heads patiently, hearing the "I walked to school along dirt roads and through the orange groves and it was pouring, no one gave us a ride" speech coming. The same kind of speech every generation of parents gives every generation of children: "twenty miles in the snow, in the desert, to a one-room school, a classroom without air conditioning."

But I tell them this because I feel sorry for them. It did rain a lot more, and so the larger drainage ditches along the side of the road, where we did walk because there were no sidewalks yet — those ditches were full of water that kept us company, gurgling and swirling companionably; in my mind, it was as close to Anne of Green Gables as I would get. Susan of the Orange Groves.

But those knee-high ditches weren't something you could lose yourself in. For that, my brothers and sister and all our friends had the flood control channel. Our big crick.

It was a huge gash in the red clay dirt of that field. The water came down from the Box Springs Mountains and was funneled into this channel, which paralleled the railroad tracks for several miles. Eventually, I figured, the water ended up in the Santa Ana River, but we weren't sure.

All we knew was it was ours. This crick belonged to my neighborhood, and we marked it our own. The sides of the ditch were very steep, about twenty feet down, and we slid on our shoes and our denimed butts, daring each other to make running starts, until we'd carved our own trails down to the mossy water. (There was a dangerous path, very stark and precipitous, and a meandering one for sissies.)

The water roared through in those rainy winters, foaming and turbulent and chocolate brown, and no one went near it, because it meant certain death. We watched it from the street then, where it rushed under the avenue carrying trash and wood and branches during severe storms.

But in summer it was a small, meandering creek, only a trickle by August and September. A few pools had formed in the deeper depressions, and the golden silt of decomposed mica and granite made lovely shallows at the edges. I could imagine the treasure a fairy would find if she collected all those tiny flakes of gold.

Were there fish? I seem to remember some, once, in a rainy spring. But I could be imagining them, too. I know animals drank there, but not the deer and foxes of my favorite stories. More like coyotes and skunks and feral cats and possums.

But if I squinted, the shopping cart someone had abandoned, covered now by grass deposited by spring floods, turned into a shaggy mammoth lingering by the water.

I made boats out of leaves. My brothers and the other neighborhood kids, mostly boys, leapt kamikaze-style from the arroyo's edges, threw dirt clods at each other rather than skipping nice round stones, and excavated huge caves in the banks. We spent hours at our crick, me always dreaming of fish and gold, them shouting and muddying the barely-there stream with bare feet.

The railroad tracks smelled of sulfur, and when trains came, we peered up at the cars from the ditch. In the vacant lot, spring brought wild mustard in yellow clouds, then wild oats as tall as we were, green that we tunneled through to get to the arroyo. At its edges, wild tobacco and a lone pepper tree were the only green.

Teenagers owned the pepper tree, where we found broken beer bottles and Boone's Farm empties. Sometimes the shards of glass glittered in the water of the ditch, treasure we collected carefully. If a stray blue bottle was broken, I was thrilled with the sapphire I imagined was real.

And later I sat under that pepper tree with my friends, watching the smaller kids slide down the trails into the arroyo, watching the apartments replace the orange groves and the canal deemed dangerous covered over with cement. Our elementary school was fenced off then, and instead of crossing the tracks and then the ditch when our parents sent us to the store for last-minute items, we had to go around on the avenue, looking down into the ditch, which was always dry now, since the rains didn't come as often.

It was dangerous. Finally the ditch itself was made into a flood control channel of concrete, slanted walls and a flat bottom featuring a trickle of water down the center. Chainlink fence around it. The field plowed. The tree gone.

There is nothing now. Even the concrete channel was thought a risk. The entire pathway for the water, rainwater or excess from the neighborhoods above, is underground.

When I show my kids my old neighborhood, only a few miles

from where we live now, I point to cement and wire and still the railroad tracks. They try to see what I am talking about. A ditch. Steep trails that kept some of our knee skin when we fell. Convoluted bottom that held water almost all year. A pepper tree with dangling leaves like rooster tails.

My kids loved to play in the sprinklers when they were little, loved the Slip 'n Slide and the baby pool. Just like I did. They love it when I take them to nearby mountains, to a stream, or to the city lake to feed the geese. More people in the city have pools now, and my kids have friends who invite them to swim. They love the water, will swim for hours, and they come home with eyes rimmed by chlorine but bodies and souls comforted by wetness.

But they don't have a wild place that is only theirs, water that comes from the sky and then the hills and along the earth. They don't have a place where no one else would want to go, a territory only they could transform.

Their lives are so different from mine, their stories to their children will be so different from my father's to me, from the stories I try to tell them when I drive along the concrete that erased our place.

I am not saying my father's crick was a magical place. He went hungry sometimes, and his life was hard. And my arroyo was frightening sometimes, with mean teenagers and wild dogs and smoggy heat that shrouded the length of the fields like a malevolent veil.

It is impossible to compare our childhoods. I'm certain that all parents, mine included, find that same impossibility when they hear me talk about my own childhood, because they knew nothing of what we did. But often I feel that my children have lost out because they don't have a ditch, the necessity to make their own crick, or the freedom to wander through the vacant lot with their friends and sit for hours carving a cavern in an arroyo with their feet in a few inches of water edged by fool's gold.

ELIZABETH STROUT

 The Swimming Pool

My father was tall. His shoes, in the glinty gravel, could have belonged to a giant. I saw them through the sparkle of water drops as I floated on my back in the section of the pool called Perch. My father wore a suit and tie, and in the summer sun he stood, his hands in his pockets, his suit coat bunched back lightly at the hips. Frog-kicking, spreading my arms out and down, I moved my way along, my father's huge shoes in sight.

"I 'spect you can do it," he said when I stepped from the pool and stood shivering. He meant he thought I could pass the test required to be able to swim in the deeper section of the pool, called Salmon. I must have been eight years old at the time. "Maybe I'll try tomorrow," I said. But as soon as my father went back to his office, I asked the lifeguard if I could take the test for Salmon. The lifeguard watched, his arms crossed, as I swam on my back the length of Perch. While I had asked my father to come to the pool to watch the dress rehearsal, I was afraid to take the actual test in front of him. It was not his displeasure I feared, if I failed — I don't imagine he would have experienced any displeasure. I imagine, in fact, he would have shrugged and told me to try again another day. But I would have felt, I think, an almost unbearable level of shame to fail in front of my father. I passed into Salmon that day, and a week later I could swim in Shark. That's where the big kids were, and the diving board.

The university swimming pool seemed to me to be big, and

old, and comfortable with itself. It was surrounded by a tall wire fence, and behind the fence, near Shark, there were trees. On a breezy day these leaves would rustle, and if a quick summer thunderstorm was on its way, they would show the pale reticulation of their undersides. Sometimes a leaf, or a twig, floated in the pool. Back then, I always swam under water with my eyes open, and I would swim deep down in Shark, so that the sounds became more and more muffled. I would swim along the bottom, looking at the old tile pieces, picking up any coin or bottle cap that might be down there, and then kick up to the surface, the sun getting brighter through the water, and then breaking through, the whistle of the lifeguard or the shouts of children or the *thunk* of the diving board as someone jumped hard emerging with a clarity of sound.

My father was a parasitologist at the University of New Hampshire, and during the years I'm speaking of, when I was seven, eight, nine, and ten, his office was in Nesmith Hall. This was an old building with a large front lawn, and since his office was in a sort of half basement, the windows looked out directly onto the lawn. I could squat down in my wet bathing suit and call to him through the open window. In my memory, he was always glad to see me, but I know too that he was often distracted, his mind frequently somewhere else.

At that time my father was on twelve-month appointment, which meant he worked through the summer. Every summer weekday I would go with him into town, either riding on the back baskets of his bicycle or, when I was old enough, riding my own bicycle. He went to his office, I went to the swimming pool. There was always that little taste of chlorine on my lips; the tips of my blond hair would turn green from it. The swimming pool was where I wanted to be, and whenever I learned something new, a different way to roll over under water, to dive without holding my nose, my father was the one I wanted watching me. I felt sad on the days it rained, as though I had been shut out of a sparkling mansion filled with sunlit rooms.

I don't remember my father ever once getting into what he called the "cesspool." But he did love the water. He loved being on the water, especially the ocean. Any kind of boat ride seemed to give him pleasure. And he loved to fish. He had a few men he would go fishing with, and sometimes he took me along. Three men sitting in a small outboard motorboat, and very seldom was a fish pulled in. One day a man named Jack — who liked to collect old glass bottles — suddenly said to me, "Stop talking so much, you're scaring the fish away." I sat silently on the pile of rope at the front of the boat, and then leaned forward and whispered to my father to ask if that was true: could the fish really hear me that far under the water? "No," he said, shaking his head, "you're all right."

But I never really liked being on the water, the way my father did. I liked being in the water, moving through it, having it all around me. I was not an especially strong swimmer, or one who learned to swim early; I had my fears. But I loved being in the swimming pool at the university, and those summer days spent there are bound up with my father, who would come by on a break if I asked him to. I needed him to see what the latest thing was I could do, whether it was swimming on my back in Perch or, later, a somersault off the diving board. My father would stand there in his suit, the only person not in bathing attire.

The pool was not far from my father's office, and at four o'clock, in order to avoid crossing the main street, which included corners of busy traffic, I would take a path around behind the dairy barn, under a bridge by the railroad tracks, and arrive at my father's office, dripping wet. If he still had work to do, I would play on the lawn out front, trying out my cartwheels, or trying to whistle through a blade of grass, or looking for a four-leaf clover, which I don't believe I ever found. Sometimes I would go inside and sit on the wooden swivel chair in front of his big wooden desk, where he let me play with anything I found in his top desk drawer.

The thing that intrigued me the most was a kind of red pencil that could be sharpened, not by a sharpener, but by peeling down the red skin, allowing the waxy red tip to become longer. I drew pictures on lined piper for him, and always he would say, "Oh, that's nice." His office was cool and dark, shaded by the trees outside, and it smelled of sawdust and chickens. Across the hall was a lab, and in the lab were chickens, and mice, and sometimes he would let me go in there with him, and I would watch while he injected the chickens with long needles. In the refrigerator were test tubes and petri dishes, and I took this world to be completely normal, as children do.

Sometimes, if I was left alone at his desk while he worked in the lab, a lab assistant or a student might come in and tell me perhaps I shouldn't be peeling back that red pencil or using so much paper. But my father always showed up and said easily, "Oh, no, it's fine." At work he wore a white lab coat over his suit. In the pockets would be peppermint LifeSavers, and in his desk drawer Licorice Nibs. "Sure," he would say when I asked for one. Sometimes he handed me coins and told me to run over and get myself an ice cream cone. Barefoot, I would walk back under the railroad bridge and get my ice cream at the dairy barn. I got chocolate: my favorite, and his.

In the vast terrain of memory, many things live. The poet Louise Glück has said, "We look at life once, in childhood; the rest is memory." There is much to look at once; and the sunlit lawns, the sparkle of the pool's water, the red pencil's thick, oily line on paper, the bottom of a soggy, chocolate-soaked waffle cone — all these things seem to present to me, in middle age, the most innocent part of my childhood. They have come to represent, in fact, what I call joy. What I call hope. There are times when we need to remember the feelings of joy and hope. And I think it is not only what we "look at once, in childhood" that determines our memories, but who, in that childhood, looks at us.

Children love to be watched. "Watch this, watch this," you can hear at any playground, any swimming pool, any back yard where there are children. It's as though we don't exist until we are seen through someone's eyes, and the Powers That Be, those adults who make the rules, are the eyes in which we most desire to be seen. It was this my father gave me, the eyes of nonjudgment (even while I judged myself harshly through my own), the willingness to stand in his suit beneath the summer sun and wait while I swam the length of Perch. Or to nod when I dove for the first time off the diving board. And when, the final summer I lived in that pool, I discovered I could do a somersault flip off the diving board, it was my father I wanted as a witness. He agreed to stop by in the afternoon, and there he was, walking across the sand in his big, grown-up shoes.

"Watch this," I said, walking onto the diving board. "Watch this." And then I couldn't do it. In fact, I never did a somersault off a diving board again. I can only think that it mattered too much to me, that my audience was too precious for me to take that chance of failing. And so my father returned to work with his pleasant, distracted gaze. "It's okay," he said. "It's really okay."

 Childhood

One evening my daughter came to pick me up from the country; I had been expecting her for several hours. Almost as soon as she came through the door I asked if she knew how potatoes look before they are dug out of the ground. She wasn't sure. Then I will show you in the morning before we head back to the city, I told her.

I had begun to harvest my potato crop the day before. In the spring I planted five varieties: my favorite, Yellow Finn, Yukon Gold, Peruvian Purple, Irish white, and red new. Even though the summer had been chilly and there was morning shade from the large oak at the front of the garden, the potatoes came up quickly and developed into healthy plants. Jose, who helps me in the garden, had shoveled an extra collar of humus around each plant, and I was delighted as each of them began to bloom. It had been years since I planted potatoes. I planted them in the garden I'd previously devoted to corn, because I have a schedule that often means I am far away from my garden at just the time my corn becomes ripe. Having sped home to my garden three years in a row to a plot of overmatured, tasteless corn, I decided to plant potatoes instead, thinking the worst that could happen, if I was delayed elsewhere, would be a handful of potatoes nibbled by gophers or moles.

I had been dreading going back to the city, where I had more things to do than I cared to think about; I sat in the swing on the deck thinking hard about what would be my last supper in the country. I had bought some green peas from the roadside stand a few miles from my house, chard and kale were flourishing a few steps from my door, and I had brought up corn from a small hopeful planting in a lower garden. Tasting the corn, however, I discovered it had, as I'd feared, given up its sweetness and turned into starch. Then I remembered my potatoes! Grabbing a shovel, I went out to the garden and began to dig. The experience I had had digging the potatoes, before turning them into half of a delicious meal, was one I wanted my daughter to know.

After boiling, I ate my newly dug potatoes, several small Yellow Finns and two larger Peruvian Purples, with only a dressing of butter. Organic butter with a dash of sea salt — that reminded me of the butter my mother and grandmother used to make. As I ate the mouth-watering meal, I remembered them sitting patiently beside the brown or creamy white churn, moving the dasher up and down in a steady rhythmic motion until flecks of butter appeared at the top of the milk. These flecks grew until eventually there was enough butter to make a small mound. We owned a beautiful handcrafted butter press. It was sometimes my job to press its wooden carving of flowers into the hardening butter, making a cheerful and elegant design.

In the morning, just before packing the car for the ride to the city, I harvested an abundance of Chardonnay grapes, greenish silver and refreshingly sweet, a bucket of glistening eggplants, an armful of collards and chard and kale, some dark green and snake-like cucumbers, plus a small sack of figs and half a dozen late-summer peaches. Then I took my daughter out to the neat rows of potatoes, all beginning to turn brown. Using the shovel to scrape aside the dirt, I began to reveal, very slowly and carefully, the golden and purple potatoes that rested just beneath the plants. She was enchanted. It's just like . . . it's just like . . . she said. It's just like finding gold, I completed her thought. Yes! she said, her eyes wide.

Though my daughter is now thirty-one, her enthusiasm reminded me of my own when I was probably no more than three. My parents, exemplary farmers and producers of fine produce in garden and field, had enchanted me early in just this same way. As I scraped dirt aside from another potato plant and watched as my daughter began to fill her skirt with our treasure, I was taken back to a time when I was very young, perhaps too young even to speak. The very first memory I have is certainly preverbal; I was lifted up by my father or an older brother, very large and dark and shining men, and encouraged to pick red plums from a heavily bearing tree. The next is of going with my parents, in a farm wagon, to a watermelon patch that in memory seems to have been planted underneath pine trees. A farmer myself now, I realize this couldn't have been true. It is likely that to get to the watermelon patch we had to go through the pines. In any case, and perhaps this was preverbal as well, I remember the absolute wonder of rolling along in a creaky wooden wagon that was pulled by obedient if indifferent mules, arriving at a vast field, and being taken down and placed out of the way as my brothers and parents began to find watermelon after watermelon and to bring them back, apparently, as gifts for me! In a short time the wagon was filled with large green watermelons. And there were still dozens more left to grow larger, in the field! How had this happened? What miracle was this?

As soon as they finished filling the wagon, my father broke open a gigantic melon right on the spot. The "spot" being a handy boulder as broad as a table that happened to reside there, underneath the shady pines, beside the field. We were all given pieces of its delicious red and thirst-quenching heart. He then carefully, from my piece, removed all the glossy black seeds. If you eat one of these, he joked, poking at my protruding tummy, a watermelon just like this will grow inside you.

It will? My eyes were probably enormous. I must have looked shocked.

Everyone laughed.

If you put the seed into the ground, it will grow, said an older brother, who could never bear to see me deceived. That's how all of these watermelons came to be here. We planted them.

It seemed too wonderful for words. *Too incredible to be believed.* One thing seemed as astonishing as another. That a watermelon could grow inside me if I ate a seed, and that watermelons grew from seeds put in the ground!

When I think of my childhood at its best, it is of this magic that I think. Of having a family that daily worked with nature to produce the extraordinary, and yet they were all so casual about it, and never failed to find my wonderment amusing. Years later I would write poems and essays about the way growing up in the country seemed the best of all possible worlds, regardless of the hardships that made getting by year to year, especially for a family of color in the South half a century ago, a heroic affair.

 Sitting

I want to ask my mother what she saw all the days she sat six floors up on her balcony these last years of her long life, watching people passing below in the streets she walked as a little girl, streets once wide and boundless as the universe Saturday afternoons with her mother Freeda by the hand, their reflections gliding across the window of the A&P, headed up Homewood Avenue, headed for Frankstown Avenue, people to smile back at who nodded or spoke or smiled at her mother or paused and spoke to the pair of them just as it had happened other Saturdays, a hand patting her olive-oil shiny braids, her shoulder, perhaps Mrs. So and So's smother-ing perfume then brisk, dry lips scratching her cheek, her little girl's name said by a person who stops them as if her name's just been invented, the three of them, her mother, herself, the one they meet in front of Mellon Bank or Colombo Bros. Hardware Store or maybe the Belmar show just before they cross Franks-town, beholding the name as if it's never been uttered before in this world until the three of them discover it each Saturday after-noon, pleased again by the wonder of it, delighted she owns it and they can say it, celebrate it when they meet on the street all the Saturdays to come my mother could tell me about if I could ask her and I want to ask her except what she sees when she stands and peers over the steel wall enclosing her balcony is her failing body mirrored in streets failing as fast as she is — *faster* the unnat-ural unthinkable but true fact — she might very well outlive the

Homewood streets just as she outlived my nameless siblings, twins, a boy stillborn, a girl expiring after a few hours, and bear witness again to the last, dismal, worn-out signs of vitality ebbing away. Why would I ask my mother to confirm what's plain as day for my own eyes to see. We both know the answer, don't we. Because she is the mother. I am the son, and the habit of turning to her, of seeking comfort in her arms, is too old to break. I am afraid for her. Her body's slow, painful unraveling. How it can tyrannize her spirit. The streets an obstinate, unforgiving reminder of how everything ends and ending's not pretty.

Here is what I ask instead. For one more time at the round oak table against the wall of her apartment furthest from the balcony door, drinking coffee together before most people out of bed and the streets below quiet as milk. What we chat about won't matter, too early for chatting anyway, I'd be content glancing about the room committing its memories to memory, finding my sister and brothers, nieces and nephews, myself, relatives of my mother's generation and their mothers and fathers, aunts and uncles, the oldest scattered, lost, long gone in photos, artifacts arrayed, arranged on the furniture, in their particular places, holding distinctive attitudes and postures they'll hold or rather maintain only as long as we look and they look back, displaying to each other shared likenesses, the poses that fill the silent reaches of my mother's apartment with a family. I'm content to think quietly such a thought and others unspeakable and listen to my mother's spoon stir into her mug sweet powder sprinkled from a pink lo-cal packet and Carnation evaporated milk poured from a red-and-white can or her voice thinking aloud about what she's heard lately on TV or read in the newspaper or someone's said on an all-night talk show, gathering help to get herself starting to talk because she's shy about her own voice, her musings, fears, worries, her opinions, even after being on the planet four fifths of a century she still dismisses what she has to say as most likely insignificant, yet no doubt about it, she also honors and guards fiercely the responsibility of her words, devotes herself to the necessity of voicing them artfully, convincingly, since they circle around and through the people she loves, and they, the words and people, are all she has, the Big World beyond her two rooms only rumors and a sad curiosity invisible until it filters through the lives of her people, her words about them, the prism the world must pass through, like light to be colored and viewed.

On her good days I imagine my mother dreaming the streets and her dreams are what happens in the streets below, the way she used to dream me home safely by sitting up and waiting for me to stumble in, no matter how late the hour back in those younger, fast days when I couldn't get enough of the street. Fuck it, I'd say at some point during nights drinking and hanging out and hitting on the ladies. If she wants to stay awake till three A.M., that's her damned, stubborn, silly business. My business right here on this stool taking care of whatever business I'm big and bad enough to get into, downing another shot of Seagram's Seven and nip of Iron City, deeper and deeper into the music and noise and dark, understanding a little more why some nights my father never made it home till dawn, understanding why my mom warned me, steered me away from this sweet, sloppy shit for as long as she could. Beginning, as I wondered what shapes the darkness might trick or treat out of itself, beginning to forgive my father — as if he cared or needed my forgiveness then when he was alive any more than he needs it now dead and in his grave — didn't he always declare he was a grown man and took his choices, paid his dues — forgive him for leaving one day and never coming back home. My own anger and guilt and pride and selfishness and pleasure hopelessly entangled with his, with hers, with the pair of them, my mother and father stuck together, unstuck, year after year, then one night when just me, my mother, and my four siblings left, I stayed out in the street till no place to go but home, pushing the limit till it wasn't night and not even dawn when I arrived home from partying, not slipping in, not tiptoeing, not slinking and creeping around, but standing taller than my absent father and looking down at a smallish, exhausted woman curled in a chair who wouldn't raise her eyes to me, didn't comment on the stinking cloud of booze, cigarette smoke, and nastiness I must have brought in the door with me, just sat in her nightgown with the housecoat wrapped around it, her bare feet in the chair's lap, squashed-back bedroom slippers on the linoleum, not bothering to ask, Where have you been, boy, not a glance up nor a challenge, shout, threat, or tears. I'd worn her out, but hadn't won, hadn't proved a goddamn thing, really, only that I could be the person she was counting on me not to be, disappointing her as she'd hoped I wouldn't, prayed I couldn't, but she must have suspected all along the moment was coming and in spite of anticipating the worst, didn't change, couldn't lose since she'd never held back, never stinted, never regretted lavishing her love on me so she couldn't lose, but I'd betrayed my love for her, if not betrayed, compromised it at the very least, towering over her in the small bare room on Copeland Street where the fatherless family had landed, me standing there in the middle of the floor, arms crossed over my chest daring to call myself a man because she'd loved me enough to set herself up for just this disappointing moment, this willful, phony little triumph of mine because I took it upon myself to teach my mother a lesson.

She'd sit up and wait and dream me home safely, and sooner or later I'd arrive in spite of myself. Ungrateful. Hating the visible wear and tear she'd endured denying herself a decent night's sleep. At my core a hollowness (or anger) where my heart should have helped me understand what I didn't, couldn't yet, and probably not to this day understand except to regret the hollowness more and wish that I could, guided by her example but in my own fashion, give to others as she gave to me, layer after layer of giving like yarn forming a ball around the vacancy at its center, her giving allowing me to grow, to stretch, binding me tighter and stronger with string she could spin from some inexhaustible source within herself, helping me hold together around the empty needle's eye she could not penetrate and I can't enter either.

The image is awkward, as awkward as I am finding words for my feelings and lack of feeling, let alone words for my mother's emotions. The image of myself as a neatly wound ball of yarn with a hole at its center and my mom as a sort of magic spider implodes, the pinpoint hollowness inside swallows everything around it, and I understand the reversal, the wipeout must have been hidden inside the words from the instant they were conceived, maybe even the reason the image was born, hungry for its turn to collapse, to take back words, shut them up, sweep them down the black hole where everything returns and emerges and returns. For no reason. In no particular order. Mother to son. Son to father. Mother to father to son. Unscheduled exchanges. Not a circle completing itself, always loose ends, loose, raggedy, orphaned threads, bloody signs left behind at each old site of attachment and separation.

I know my mother didn't speak to me on the morning I was trying to prove a point, did prove a point but not the one I believed I was making, and know, thank goodness, she must have started talking to me again because here we are this morning, chattering now. Maybe she didn't speak to me that whole first day or fragment of day, but sooner or later she'd picked up where we'd left off before I walked out the door one night and didn't return till long past the hour I desired to return. The hour I could reasonably assume weariness would push her into a numbed drowsiness that would serve as sleep even if she continued to worry and will herself awake. Staying out past that hour I knew I'd be doling out a dose of pain to my mother. Pushing her to the point of pain and then farther, going about my partying with no remorse, perhaps with extra satisfaction, as if she deserved discomfort, earned it by being susceptible to it, earned it by being stubborn and unreasonable, keeping up a habit begun when I was in my early teens of waiting till I arrived home before she goes to sleep. Pain I told myself that hurt me as much or more than her. Which was partly true and also a perversely gratifying refrain since I borrowed it from her, words, if not spoken aloud, implied during rare physical punishments she inflicted on me when I was little, pain I wouldn't have been able to bear otherwise. Hurting her one night and morning to learn how not to let her hurt me. Disciplining her to undo hurt she inflicted upon herself. Hurting her so she doesn't hurt herself unnecessarily because I was okay, dammit, fine, grown, didn't need her hurt dogging me, hurting me while I was out trying to have fun. It's all pretty raw still, I guess. What was unfolding that morning hurt us both, no doubt, hurts this instant as I recite the evil word *hurt* over and over, the word changing in quality, quantity, significance, shrinking into itself, exploding boundaries, rising in degree of difficulty with each repetition, each performance.

If she sits on the plastic lawn chair pulled up beside a matching table topped by its ghetto of crowded, scraggly potted plants, the chair stationed at the end of the balcony a sliding glass door opens onto, the chair we can see through the door's pale, nearly transparent curtain when we're drinking coffee at the round oak table, if she's in that chair, my mother spends most of her time leaning down and peeking through an opening that runs between balcony railing and a chest-high barrier bolted to the concrete floor. Since the barrier's a solid sheet of metal and the steel tubing rail fastened above it too high to see over when she's settled on the Kmart stacking chair, it's either stand up and look over the railing or bend down to the slot if she wants to check out the street. From the chair if you push it back a bit from the barrier or from inside the apartment if you draw back the glass door's curtain, you can view a line of steep hills opposite the senior citizens' low-rise, hills clustered and climbing each other, crowded with houses and housing projects and apartment buildings, waves of hills receding finally to form the dark, undulating horizon where Homewood-Brushton's highest houses and trees meet the sky. Enough big trees remain to turn the helter-skelter hillsides green in spring and summer, transform them to a motley tapestry of golds and reds in fall. Dropping off precipitously from the hills and stretching to the left, enormous swatches of Pittsburgh spread out, punctuated by thrusting landmarks whose names I know and spires and towers I've seen all my life but couldn't name if you paid me. On clear days a bluish haze to the west, toward Oakland and Downtown, the three rivers, Allegheny, Ohio, Monongahela, converging at the Golden Triangle. Frankstown Avenue's steep rise in the opposite direction levels at East Hills, some of Homewood-Brushton's best houses folded into the steepness before the edge of the suburb, a panorama of city over which planes too far away to hear sail regularly so it must be a favorite flight path to the Greater Pittsburgh airport in Carnegie.

From her chair outside on the balcony on the top floor of what I've been told is the tallest residential building in Homewood my mom can daydream at the sky, gaze at the backdrop of hills in the middle distance, but she cannot tend to the business in the streets below unless she stands or bows her head like someone peering into a microscope or praying and peeks through the slot running the length of the guard wall some kind architect devised so old birds like her don't tumble from the nest.

I feel myself in her body, the congenital ache we share, hunched over blessedly unaware of straining muscles in the lower back, muscles and ligaments and nerves forgotten until she straightens up and they spasm and scream, but nothing hurts at first, just a little stiffness as she leans down to peer through the slot, concentrating on the boy who hops down from the last step of the yellow school bus, same stop, same time, same hop five days a week. A boy about the age Brian, Tameka's oldest, was last year. She must cross him — that brown, bouncy, in-a-hurry boy — at the red light when he listens to her but most days he darts, ignoring her, his eyes she hopes paying attention to the traffic on Frankstown, not heavy like in Frankstown's heyday but picking up at the hour the school bus stops not quite at the corner, still, enough cars to worry about since it only takes one and there's always one it seems ready and willing to do a terrible thing, engine gunned, the roar, horn, brakes squealing and sometimes glass shattering, metal crunched and twisted, the soft, giving sound of flesh lost in shattering explosions, she hears them daily, gunshots, reports of dying, hears cars rushing through the night driven by angry men, by boys not much older than the one whose hand she takes in her mind, when he'll let her take it, and crosses him on green, steps him up on the far curb, turns him left, past the fools and lost souls and nothing-better-to-dos loafing outside Mason's bar, then crosses him through the vacant lot alongside Mason's where they killed a boy, the boy whose shape, in spite of the darkness, she could almost make out from the balcony, lying in the thick weeds the city came and cut a few days after the boy shot down, after a night cops stalked in pairs through the jungle where pitiful souls squat to do their business after dark, where they sleep and eat and fight and curse, mostly men back there but some sorry women too, cops flashing flashlights and big spotlights from humming trucks parked on the sidewalk. She watched two of them, plainclothes detectives, walking slowly, zigzag, like they know better than to be where they find themselves, not in any hurry to reach the lot's far end, the alley blacker than the lot that cuts behind row houses and apartment buildings black too at that time of night, one cop in a long dark leather jacket, the other a bulky trench coat, collar turned up, took their good time, even with other cops everywhere, and their own guns out and flashlights lit, strolling zigzag to the edge of the lot, then stop and peer up and down, around the corners of buildings this side of the alley like bookends holding in the lot's emptiness, the men not taking a single step further, as if the back alley's a boiling river.

She crosses the boy in daylight, on a path tamped down in weeds grown thick again since they were clipped by fellows who came in a truck, one riding a loud mower, unchained and ramped down from the truck's flatbed, two with rakes and old-timey sickles chop-chop-chopping weeds, taking away with them when the truck rolled off she prayed the dead boy's shape that had been pressed into the weeds, so maybe it's better now, safer now she squeezes the boy's hand before she lets go and he bends to get the key from a box or coffee can or flowerpot beside the two steps into his house, front steps or back alley steps she doesn't know what to call them, watching while he unlocks the door, opens it, steps inside, and her deep exhale could be the door wheezing shut safely behind him.

Is that how you dream the streets, Mom, how you dreamed me, dream lives for the people you observe each day from your sixth-floor perch, here where your God has assigned you, or some might say deserted you, no mercy for your bad back or your crippled legs or your astronomical blood pressure or gout or the cancer burrowing into your colon until it decides you had misery enough already so crawled off to murder a healthier host, no pity on your hyperactive sinuses or the burn, stiffness, pinch, and sleep-stealing scourge of arthritis. The same God, you'd be quick to remind me, shushing me, scolding me with your eyes, the God who you'd say wrapped his hand around yours and guided you to this station, led you here to spend the last days of your life in exactly the spot you would have chosen for yourself you'd say, for your last days if you could have figured it out. But of course you couldn't have, not without his mercy and guidance. No, you weren't prepared for any of this, neither the good nor the awful things, nor could you have guessed in any way shape or form what life would require of you, except you depended on his sweet everlasting love you'd say, wouldn't you, and that was preparation enough, enough understanding, enough peace. More than you or any lost soul had any right to expect.

You'd answer something like that no matter what I asked, wouldn't you, Mom. I understand faith is an answer to any question I can pose. The unshakable faith I've learned to admire, even envy. In you nothing that happens in the world or spirit raises real doubts. You could be beaten up, beaten down, extinguished, and still not lose your trust in a plan, a purpose no matter how long, how much you must suffer without the slightest explanation of why. I'm not suggesting that you can be hurt without being hurt. Just the opposite. And far from being meek or complacent or resigned, you fight. You don't deny hurt, you're not impervious to suffering, you resist the suffering you and others are forced to endure, the suffering and mayhem I find incomprehensible except as a sign of chaos, of no God, or of abandonment, even though I've known better for a good long while than to assume we were meant to be cared for or loved in the first place. I'm proud of your way of fighting fire with fire, your hot anger like the blazes set to save a vast, blazing forest. I steal that fire. Try to imagine faith's presence in you, wonder if you try to imagine its absence in me. Is that how stories begin. Why they turn to ashes.

LOIS-ANN YAMANAKA
 JohnJohn's World

So silent, I think.

He stands near the white gingers, pulls the blossoms petal by petal from their lush bouquets. He throws handfuls in the air like confetti caught in the trade winds. A quiet joy, my JohnJohn, surrounded for a moment by the intense fragrance of flowers, the white shower of ginger falling around him.

And I think, "He loves me. He loves me not."

And I know: He loves me. Forty-three times a day.

From some psychology journal, I know the human animal needs forty-three hugs a day to survive.

No one has ever held me in a full embrace forty-three times a day like JohnJohn does. Doesn't know that a hug should end when a hug should end. It's his autism, I think. What Bruno Bettelheim called a lack of social awareness and social relationships.

But something passes back and forth between us again and again. I feel it inside me like the surging of kinetic waves. Forty-three times a day.

It is another Saturday. JohnJohn holds my hand as we wait in line at the supermarket. He looks at all of the Mylar balloons bobbing in the air-conditioned draft at the checkout. Today he wants the balloons. All of them.

I know he might throw a fabulous autistic tantrum as soon as I say the word *no*. So I try not to panic. We need to cross "groceries" off our never-ending to-do list. I try to ignore him. I put the celery and cheese slices on the conveyor belt. Coffee, frozen chicken, cat food.

He lets go of my hand. "Ba-noon," he says, a whisper at first.

I acknowledge him with a nod for the language that I long for, my prayers since his diagnosis filled with begging God for JohnJohn's words.

A bag of apples and a dozen eggs glide away from us.

He steps away from me.

"JohnJohn —" I call him.

He tries to gather up the balloons tied to racks of the *Enquirer* and *Woman's Day*, pulls and yanks at the ribbons with tiny jingle bells on their ends. A Happy Birthday balloon gets away.

The entire supermarket goes silent.

Then JohnJohn screams.

Someone gasps. Women stare and pull their own children closer to them as I struggle to get screaming and crying, feet-kicking, back-arching JohnJohn out of the market. A security guard steps toward us. The clerk shakes his head at my abandoned shopping cart full of groceries, the spin of apples on a conveyor belt.

In JohnJohn's world, I can afford to buy him every balloon on every trip to the market. In JohnJohn's world, he takes all of the shiny balloons home to our yard full of white ginger blossoms and lets all of them go. Watches them spin their silver way in the trade winds, over treetops and rooftops, out of the valley. A moment of beauty, his silent freedom.

꧁

There was a speech pathologist who said to me, "I think the Department of Education is doing more than its share in providing services for John. My schedule is very full." She saw him for fifteen minutes on Mondays, Wednesdays, and Fridays. I was asking for Tuesdays and Thursdays. He was still preverbal.

I heard the whispering: "John is very low-functioning."

There was a special education teacher who slapped him across the face, dragged him across the floor, then put her knee on his back. "It was an unintentional block," the principal told me. "John hit her first."

I listened to their test results: "Cognitive understanding of language: 23 months. Emerging skills: 2 years, 9 months. Cognitive verbal expressive ability: 23 months. Emerging skills: 2 years, 8 months." He was ten years old.

There was a therapeutic aide from the Department of Health who read romance novels while JohnJohn ate his lunch alone. "John needs to use a napkin to wipe his face at lunch," she told me. "Do you let him use his hand at home?"

※

His silence screams from their memos:

> To: Principal
> Fr: Room 44
> Cc: VP and parents
> Re: John

John bolted out of the classroom. He began to hit and bite as I led him to the assembly. I have scratches on my face and neck, and bruises and bite marks on my arms. John raged for one hour and thirty-eight minutes.

※

> To: Principal
> Fr: Room 44
> Cc: VP, SSC, and parents
> Re: John's *aggressive* behavior

John lunged at Max's face. We had a hard time pulling him off. We need an emergency IEP meeting. This is now a staff and student safety issue.

To: Principal
Fr: Room 44
Cc: VP, SSC, EA, TA, and parents
Re: John's escalating *violent* behavior

John picked up a chair and threw it at me. I evacuated the other children and staff to a safe area outside. Have his parents consulted their psychiatrist to possibly increase meds?

To: Principal
Fr: Room 44
Cc: VP, SSC, Occ. T, Phys. T, Sp. T, PPT, TA, EA, and parents
Re: John's *self-mutilation*

John tore off his shirt in the middle of the field. He gouged himself repeatedly. Do I need to fill out any paperwork to document what happened?

What would JohnJohn tell me if he could?
He would tell me how light attracts light.
How light also attracts darkness.
He would tell me about forgiveness.
And then he would tell me about love.

I cannot recall my mother or father, my sisters, or anyone else in my family saying the words *I love you* to me as a child. I was told that our actions speak louder than words. It was even biblical.

I would even venture to say that no one has *ever* really loved me. It's the stuff of years of therapy, hundreds of bad poems and angst-ridden stories, suicide letters documenting names and places, and one too many soulful karaoke ballads from the pit of my bleeding heart.

I have heard the words *I love you* but know that I never *truly* believed the words spoken to me by the hometown boy in the back seat of my mother's Corolla. A friend or two in a *Beaches* moment. This man, that man. This girl, that poet. Always a cheap bottle of merlot.

And then for the first time I heard the words *I love you*.

It was Christmas morning. JohnJohn stood over me. He was five. He was singing the ABC song, a song that we sang to him over and over, praying for language to sink in through repetition and rote.

That morning he sang a child's song to me. The moment lasted the sweetest forever. It was almost a dream, the song he sang with so much love for me.

A song that he never sang again.

"I love you, JohnJohn," I said as he crawled under the covers this cold morning.

He did not look at me, but I heard him, as I would hear him again and again many times a day for the weeks, months, and years to come: "Ai yav you."

Never withholding the words *I love you* from me as many times as I needed to hear them each and every day.

JohnJohn loved his educational aide Nohea. When he could no longer manage the day loaded with sensory input, she walked with him in a calm silence.

On one of their long walks, JohnJohn looked into a room full of second-graders. The teacher, not stopping her lesson, waved him in with a broad grin.

A jar with holes punched into its cover with a chrysalis inside. A calendar.

"It will be a monarch butterfly in fourteen days," the teacher JohnJohn would call Mrs. O told the class.

JohnJohn visited her classroom every day after lunch.

Fourteen days later, a second-grade girl knocked on the door to JohnJohn's special ed classroom. She led JohnJohn and Nohea to the big field by the basketball courts.

Mrs. O's children formed a small circle around him. "The class voted," she said. "We want JohnJohn to release the butterfly." Mrs. O slowly opened the jar, then stepped toward JohnJohn.

Afraid, he backed away. Nohea placed her hands on his shoulders. "You can do it," she whispered in his ear. She took JohnJohn's hand and moved his finger toward the unfurling wings.

The butterfly stepped out of the jar and onto JohnJohn's trembling finger. It rested there, taking in the world, the sunlight, the trade winds, and JohnJohn's wide eyes as he lifted his hand to the sky for that ceremonious moment of first flight.

There are moments when I know that JohnJohn's inner world is without boundary.

When he was seven, he took the bag of yellow magnetic alphabet letters to the refrigerator as he had done many times before. But this time, one by one, I listened to the slow snap of plastic letters onto cold metal. I peered at him from behind the living room wall. JohnJohn had spelled out his first word.

U-N-I-V-E-R-S-A-L.

"Such a big and profound word, JohnJohn." I spoke with my mind, my heart, fluttering inside me. "Yes, you are *universal*. You are the moon and the stars, the oceans and the mountains, the planets and galaxies, a million constellations."

I remained still as he began to compose another word.

D-I-M-E-N-S-I-O-N-A-L.

"Yes, you are multi*dimensional*," I told him, "layers upon layers of depth and knowledge, all inside of you, my little JohnJohn."

I held him close to me when he was done, breathing in the sweet of his neck and hair. Hug number twenty-five.

We left his words there for years, the mold and dust of time on yellow plastic. It was a reminder of his message to all of us:

Universality, all of us here for a reason, the universality of the human experience no matter what our circumstance.

Dimensionality, all of us multifaceted beings of mind, body, soul, and light.

Daylight seeps through the shower trees, the flutter of rice sparrows in and out of shadows. A light rain slants in the northerly trade winds. White and yellow ginger blooms through late summer.

It is a silent world in the valley we call home.

JohnJohn loves the sky, the movement of the clouds down the Ko'olau Mountains, iridescent bubbles floating down from the top of his tree house, the butterflies that lift themselves from our purple crownflower tree.

His cousin Samantha looks down at JohnJohn from the top of the tree house. She puts the bubble wand back in the plastic bottle.

"Why is JohnJohn always covering his ears like that?" she asks me.

They would say.

Because he is.

AUTISTIC:

Hyperawareness to environmental input.

Multisensory integration deficits.

Augmented response to sound.

Stereotyped motor behavior.
Auditory overstimulation.
Failure to habituate.
Developmental delay.
Hypersensitivity.

"Why?" she asks again.
I tell her because he is our JohnJohn, my JohnJohn:
He can hear the sound of the butterfly's wings.